Caught
in the Headlights

10 LESSONS LEARNED
THE HARD WAY

Caught
in the Headlights

---

10 LESSONS LEARNED
THE HARD WAY

BARRY K. PHILLIPS

CFI
Springville, Utah

ISBN 13: 978-1-59955-167-8

Published by CFI, an imprint of Cedar Fort, Inc., 2373 W. 700 S., Springville, UT 84663
Distributed by Cedar Fort, Inc. www.cedarfort.com

LIBRARY OF CONGRESS CATALOGING-IN-PUBLICATION DATA

Phillips, Barry K., 1962–
  Caught in the headlights : ten lessons learned the hard way / Barry K.
Phillips ; with foreword by Glenn Beck.
    p. cm.
  ISBN 978-1-59955-167-8 (alk paper)
  1. Conduct of life. 2. Self-help techniques. I. Title.

BJ1581.2.P53 2008
170'.44—dc22

2008010877

Cover design by Jeremy Beal
Cover design © 2008 by Lyle Mortimer
Edited and typeset by Annaliese B. Cox

Printed in the United States of America

10 9 8 7 6 5 4 3 2 1

Printed on acid-free paper

For my wife, Susan, who let me learn these lessons
and stood by me through it all

CONTENTS

FOREWORD

I first met Barry when he started writing for my magazine, *Fusion*. I like his writing, but an entire book? Please.

Thankfully, Barry must've had my ADD in mind when he wrote this because the chapters are nice and short. I'd read a page or two, get distracted by something shiny, and then be able to pick it right back up without ever missing a beat.

But the truth is that I really like this book. It hits on some key things that most of us struggle with throughout our lives, and it does it in the way I like best: irreverent and politically incorrect.

I suspect that most of us are surprised at how difficult life can be at times. The secret that Barry has found is to learn as you go along and try to do better the next time.

And that's really what this book is all about. The more we learn, the less we have to repeat our mistakes.

The combination of humor, insight, and frank discussion sets this book apart. If we could each master the concepts laid out here, just imagine how much better off we'd be personally, not to mention the world.

If you're reading this while still standing in the bookstore, go buy it, you cheapskate. The guy's got like 800 kids; he seriously needs the cash.

That's better. Now I hope you enjoy it as much as I did.

—Glenn Beck

SETTING THE STAGE

The truth is, there are days when I can't believe I'm still alive. Not that I live such a dangerous life that assassins are after me or that I've been ravaged by a terminal disease. Nothing so traumatic. But life has been and still often is, well . . . hard. At times I'm just weary. Still, I keep waking up each morning, so I've got to do something about it. Not that I'm a victim here, far from it. Along the way there have been some great things in my life as well. Both the good and the bad, the tiring and the invigorating, bring about great challenges and opportunities for learning. I just wish I wouldn't get in my own way so much. We've all heard the saying that he who does not learn from history is destined to repeat it. I try to live by that one. If I could just turn hindsight into foresight, the journey wouldn't be so treacherous.

I suspect, like most of you, I've set out after some things that I thought I really wanted, only to find out that what I really wanted was something very different—better, as it turns out, but different. And that's what this book is about. The stuff I thought I wanted versus the stuff I really wanted or needed, or should have wanted or needed. You know, those "caught in the headlight" moments when I've realized I've been pursuing the wrong things. My guess is that you've wanted many of these same things too. You'll even find a few cartoons and poems (not that sappy chick flick kind of poem; you'll see what I mean) as we go, mostly because I like to draw and write, and also because sometimes they can drive home a point better than any other way. Hopefully, you'll find it insightful and a little

1

humorous. If you don't, well . . . tough; write your own book. Just remember I get royalties because I gave you the idea.

You are no doubt asking yourself, "What qualifies this guy to write a book?" If you weren't thinking that, you are now, so let me give you the best answer I can. Frankly, I would have written this a few years earlier were it not for that very question. I lacked the confidence to just do it. I'm not the president of a *Fortune 500* company, though I do run a few small businesses. I'm not famous, wealthy, or incredibly brilliant—an obvious point that you will see as time goes on. Then again, compared to some folks, and what they do to their own lives, maybe brilliance is a relative thing. Take Donald Trump for example—very successful from a business perspective. But his personal life is not something I'd want to emulate. And that hair of his? Please. Couldn't he just pay someone to tell him the truth once in a while? Enough about the Donald. As to my credentials, rather than explain who I'm not, here's just a few words about who I am.

First, I am a husband of over twenty-four years—and yes, to the same woman. She's a saint for sticking with me, to be sure. I'm also the father of five children. Five great children. Five fantastic children. A slight bias? Maybe just a little. But, so far the kids are doing well. Their mother can take a great deal of credit for that, of course, but it's ME that is smart enough not to mess up all the good she does.

Professionally, I have run several companies and have written or co-written over ten training courses ranging from leadership and mentoring to problem solving and public speaking. I've taught these skills inside some of the largest and most successful companies in America. Not that I'm taking credit for their success, but the timing is startling. At least in my own mind. Then again, lots of things are startling in my mind, so that's not an unusual thing.

Where was I? Oh yes, my feeble list of qualifications. I've studied human behavior a great deal over the years and have consulted professionally in these areas. I've written for two national magazines and was editor-in-chief for one of them. I love to cook, draw, and play drums. I like long walks on the beach, the smell after a rain storm, and . . . oh, sorry—wrong list. I've had some great successes and some miserable failures and have discovered that you can learn a great deal from both. That's what makes me nervous about people who have seen only success. Too much success and not much in the failure category can be a dangerous thing. Failure is a great teacher. Not that success is bad. Are you kidding?

I like success—really, I do. Success is a good thing, but it doesn't teach you the same lessons as failure. It's that whole "well roundedness" thing they used to tell me about in college as to why studying kinematics was going to be useful in my life. But I digress. Speaking of college, I do have a bachelor's degree from a real university, not that the degree is much of a qualification. As I'm now in my early, well, more like mid-forties (I'm comfortable growing old, really I am), I've hopefully learned a few things that are worth passing on. I think my most relevant qualification is that I have just plain made more mistakes than most of you. So, those are just a few of the vast items on my list of qualifications. If needed, I'll invent—I mean disclose—more of them later on.

Oh, one more thing that you might as well know right up front. I have a conservative point of view on life and I'm a very religious man—a Christian. There, I said it and I'm proud of it. A bit of a rant is warranted here. First, this book is not about politics. The conservative viewpoint means that I believe strongly in self-reliance and personal responsibility. If you don't believe in these things, you should. Those who don't believe in them typically don't accomplish much—except a great deal of whining and blaming others. As to the Christian part, that is a critical element. It is the guiding force in who I am, what I believe, and how I behave. There are some in the "intellectual" crowd who think religion is for the simple minded. I'm astounded at that level of arrogance and narrow mindedness. To really believe that man has or will have all the answers is difficult to comprehend. To subscribe to that philosophy, you have to really believe that coincidence and happenstance are really, really common—really. It's like connecting the dots on a drawing and jumping from number three to number forty-seven and arguing that the other dots just don't matter—only three and forty-seven, because those are the dots I know the most about. So forgive me if I don't talk about "intelligent design" or the "creationist theory." It's God the Father and his Son Jesus Christ. That's who they are—they are real, and they matter.

Okay, I might be slightly opinionated. But opinions are not bad if they are based on good information, well thought out arguments, and an open mind that is still willing to entertain other points of view. Entertain does not mean waffle, just a willingness to consider and re-evaluate a position and come to a decision based on the best information available. Deep, huh? It made me tired just thinking about it. Don't worry. I won't make you think that hard too often; we'd hate to risk mental exercise for you or me. After all, we all need to save those brain cells for more important things. You know, like helping that poor man that sent you an email from Nigeria and can't get his money out of the bank without using your account to deposit the money—stuff like that.

Each chapter of this book will cover a primary topic. As I said, the topics are about stuff I went after that I thought I wanted but instead I learned what really matters while in the pursuit. I may stray a bit here and there, but stick with me. I usually get back on point somewhere along the way.

1

HAPPINESS

Pursuit 1

What I really wanted was happiness

I thought we'd better start with this subject because it is an underlying principle for everything else. Based on my premise of stuff I thought I wanted but learned better, you must think I don't want to be happy. Wrong. I do. But when I was younger, I didn't really understand what happiness was or how to get there from here. It took a great deal of time, and more trial and error than I would care to admit, but I've finally figured out how this whole happiness thing works. I didn't say I'm perfect at obtaining happiness all the time—far from it. But the formula works if I have the discipline to stick with it. So let's start with the basics. First let's look at the root word of happiness—happy. Webster's first definition is "favored by luck or fortune."

By that definition, being happy has much more to do with luck than with anything you or I do to obtain a state of being happy. We have to rely on the luck of the draw, the roll of the dice—in short, pure dumb luck. If that's true, why do so many people spend the bulk of their lives trying to do things that will make them happy? Think about it: if you are married, why did you choose your spouse? I chose my wife because I thought being with her would make me *happy* (and the fact that she didn't get physically ill in my presence was a real plus, but that's another story). Silly me—why did I worry about being happy if it was all a matter of fate? Nope. I can't accept that definition for happiness.

So what about pleasure? That must bring the happiness we are all looking for, right? Las Vegas is filled with people night after night putting that one to the test. The truth is that pleasure and true happiness have very little in common. Pleasure is short-term and rarely, if ever, leads to the long-term happiness that we're really after. Momentary pleasures more often lead to long-term misery and regret if they are done without the long-term plan in mind. Since I have brought up the subject of Las Vegas, have you seen their advertising campaign that says, "What happens in Vegas stays in Vegas"? There's your "get out of jail free" card for pleasure. No consequences because no one will tell, so no one will know. Except, of course, *you*. Oh, and *God*. Maybe a legal disclaimer for their ads would help. You know the type, like the ones at the end of pharmaceutical commercials where the potential side effects are worse than the disease you are trying to cure. It should read something like this:

> Offer valid for persons with no conscience or moral character only. In the event there is actually a God, this offer is null and void. Persons being condemned at the judgment seat to a toasty place in hell may not use this offer as a legal and binding contract. While Satan was involved in the creation of this offer, he cannot be held responsible for your actions. After all, he IS Satan. Persons repenting later may experience a shortness of breath, deep sorrow, and excessive amounts of regret. Offer intended for the use of our regular, soulless clientele only. Offer not valid where prohibited, including all aspects of your life once you return home.

Now *there* would be some truth in advertising. But it's not likely to happen. Even without it, people seeking instant gratification soon find out they are left empty. Happiness is not found through pleasure.

A common cliché is that man (by "man" I mean the generic term for mankind—not that I'm excluding women, kids, or politicians. See how politically correct I can be if I try? Don't get used to it; that doesn't happen too often). Now where was I? Oh, the cliché is that man has two primary motivators: (1) to obtain pleasure and (2) to avoid pain. We have already discussed the pitfalls of the pleasure side, and I suspect that there must be more to life than just avoiding pain. I refuse to believe that if I simply avoid bad stuff that I will be deliriously happy. Life is more complex than that. Just because someone way-back-when came up with that concept and threw it over the wall to the rest of us, doesn't mean it's true. Some clichés are true, which is why they hang around so long. But many are not true. Their longevity may be attributed to the fact that people want them to be true, or simply because it's an old saying and who am I to try to correct it?

There is certainly more to happiness than can be summed up in some trite saying. There is more to be discovered than that. I've seen a lot of people trying desperately to do whatever it takes to become happy. The interesting thing is that I've never seen anyone achieve happiness by pursuing it. To understand why that is the case, I first had to understand what the real goal is that we are all looking for.

Is the state of being happy the correct goal? It seems too fleeting and too hard to maintain for very long—at least when using the conventional definitions of the word. After searching for that pot of gold at the end of the rainbow, I discovered that my eyes were on the wrong prize. I'm really not looking for a euphoric high all the time. We've all seen people who've tried to keep that going. We usually call them alcoholics or drug addicts. Ultimately, they are also known as miserable, lonely, or dead. Not a pretty picture. I was not happy with the highs and lows of momentary euphoria. The older I became, the less palatable the roller coaster ride seemed to be. While the pleasure route has never been the road I've taken, looking for happiness in other ways has left me empty just the same.

The road I was on was tied too much to external events and tangible possessions. You know, things like accolades from others in business, a bigger house, or nicer cars. Then it hit me. What I was looking for was not happiness by standard conventions; what I really wanted can be summed up in one word—*peace*. Not just the absence of conflict, but true peace— a sense of comfort that all (or at least most) is going well in my world.

This kind of peace comes through many different ways that all tie in together. One of the most important things I found was that peace is largely determined by the relationships in my life. For example, when my relationship with my wife is going well (and, dear, it's always great, really), there is a peace that comes from that. The knot in the pit of my stomach brought on from the stresses of life seems to loosen. The funny thing is, that element of my life really has been great for me, but I didn't always fully appreciate it. I took it for granted. I kept looking for that brass ring, the next giant conquest, rather than having the perspective that new challenges are important but less important than how my relationship is going with those I care about most.

Other relationships rank up there as well. While you may have others on your list, there are some common ones that we all share. These include family (spouse, children, extended family), God, and work (boss, peers, clients). If any of those relationships are out of whack, peace is difficult to find.

Okay, there are a few others you may want to add to that list. Anyone that is in your food chain matters—the pizza delivery guy, Chinese food delivery person—you know, the other essential people in your life. Plus, the people that keep your cable or satellite feeding that signal to your TV . . . and those Internet geeks. Let's face it, you may not want to hang out with them, but every now and then you really need to have them in your life. Just make sure your relationship with them is not on the rocks. I mean, your cable going out during the Super Bowl is bad, real bad—and these people can make that happen. The power they wield is awesome. Just don't mess with them. Enough said.

Now back to the first people on the list. When your relationships are all going well, your life is going well. There may not be giddy laughter and tingling thrills all the time, but that overall sense of peace makes life worth living. There is a balance that helps you make the right choices in all aspects of life. I should note that if you pay particular attention to your relationship with God, he will ensure that you put the proper focus on the other relationships. And believe me, you don't want to forget God in the process. There's this book I read about a guy named Jonah who didn't really like God's point of view. The Lord put him in "time out" in the belly of a fish (really . . . it wasn't a whale, it was a fish—read the book again) so he could rethink the choices he had made. Peace certainly didn't come for him until he got his priorities straight.

C. S. Lewis is one of my favorite authors and social commentators. He had great insight into what life is all about. Regarding peace and happiness, he had this to say: "God cannot give us happiness and peace apart from himself, because it is not there. There is no such thing."[1]

He's right. Those who find true peace and happiness always have a strong relationship with their Creator. This book is not meant to be about religion, but facts are facts—you need God in your life to find peace. For those that struggle with your level of faith, C. S. Lewis said something that may give you a new perspective: "I believe in Christianity as I believe that the sun has risen: not only because I see it, but because by it I see everything else."[2]

The science that nonbelievers tend to put their faith in will always come up wanting. In his own battle to gain faith, Lewis simply states, "I gave in, and admitted that God was God."[3]

Peace is what it's all about. It is the anchor in tough times and the moderator in good times. Finding true peace is difficult, and keeping it requires a daily regimen. I know I got a little deep again. Sorry. But this stuff really matters. It is the key to everything else. If you don't know what you are looking for, it becomes very difficult to find. Just how to obtain peace is the subject of many chapters to come. But for this chapter, here is the lesson learned.

Lesson 1

You can't find happiness by pursing it. Peace is the goal.

So what do I do about it?

Understanding that peace is what I'm after is a vital step. But knowing that, if I can't *apply* the lesson to my life, how did it help me? Not much. So, with peace as the goal, here's the plan of attack. I'll stick with just three things to do; more than that can be too overwhelming. Again, let me give the disclaimer that I'm not perfect at this by any stretch of the imagination, but the more I apply these principles, the more peace I find.

1. *Focus on relationships.* For example, the more I think about what my wife is going through, the more I question her about *her* day and the more I try to help her in what she is doing.

A note to guys: sometimes women want to tell you stuff about their lives, but they don't necessarily want you to *do* anything about it! They just want you to listen and care. I know that's hard, because most of us male types want to fix things. Just be sure she *wants* your help before you jump in.

Okay, back to the relationship thing. When I say focus on relationships, I mean think about them and *do* something to strengthen them. If you are frustrated at work because your boss doesn't let you know how well you are or are not doing, you can actually ask him for feedback and *you* can offer up compliments on what *he* is doing. Everyone likes to know that their work is appreciated, and you can set the example for that.

2. *Spend less time on pleasure and more on things that bring peace.* I don't mean you have to give up watching sports or reading romance

novels (okay, maybe giving up on the romance novels is not such a bad thing). Just don't let them be the dominant thing in your life. Keep them in balance. Add some things into your schedule like a daily walk with your spouse—no cell phones or iPods allowed. Schedule time to play with your kids. Get involved in church activities. Just make sure your free time has meaningful things scheduled as well as just fun things.

3. *Plan, plan, plan.* You may not be a daily planner type of a person. On the other hand, you may live too much by a schedule. Either way, force yourself to take some time each week (Sunday afternoons work best for me) and think about the relationships and important things that matter most to you and make sure you schedule at least one thing (if not more) for the coming week for each relationship that will help to strengthen the bond with that person—remember God is one of those relationships to work on. Your work and other play things will easily fill in the gaps, so put those peace-oriented things on the schedule first. Just imagine looking back on your past seven days and realizing that you had done something worthwhile in each relationship you care about. Now that's a peaceful feeling.

Also, plan some *peaceful* vacations that will allow quality time with those you love. My fondest memories are not of the thrills of an amusement park but of the time spent laughing, talking, and working with those I love. I'm willing to bet those are your fondest memories as well.

If your focus is on peace rather than "happiness," you will set your goals and priorities differently because you truly want something different—something long-lasting, something better. You want peace.

Alright, it's time for one of those poetic moments I warned you about. Bear with me on this, it really does make a point.

> As we all go through this life,
> There's one trait that we share.
> We are on a common quest
> That leads us here and there.
>
> Most do not even realize
> Why we do the things we do.
> But somewhere deep inside us,
> It's happiness we each want too.

Some look for happiness in working;
Some fill their lives with sports.
Some always have bad attitudes—
Maybe too much starch in their shorts.

Some people hoard all their money
In a private safe in their closet.
And if money doesn't buy happiness,
They hope it will make a deposit.

But the path does not require riches
Or the need of power and fame.
Though many focus efforts here,
They bring emptiness just the same.

So if happiness does not come
From indulging in life's pleasures . . .
Could it be our personal relationships,
That bring it in such great measures?

Perhaps happiness can only be *given*
Through acts of kindness, large and small.
Then the key to finding true happiness
Would be to not look for it at all.

And in the process of *not* looking
And doing what you know to be right,
An inner peace is what you'll find,
Which stays with you day and night.

Notes

1. C. S. Lewis, *Mere Christianity* (New York: Harper Collins Publishers, Inc., 2001), 50.
2. C. S. Lewis, *The Weight of Glory: And Other Addresses* (New York: Harper Collins Publishers, Inc., 2001), 140.
3. C. S. Lewis, *Surprised by Joy* (Orlando: Harcourt Brace & Co., 1955), 228.

2

Self-Esteem

Pursuit 2

What I wanted was self-esteem

This one may take many of you by surprise. Self-esteem is a very important thing to have, right? In fact, our education system and even most aspects of our society are based on building self-esteem. We all want to feel good about ourselves. So what could be wrong with that? Well, plenty.

First, let's look at our formative education years and see what all this self-esteem has done. Let me preface this with one of my favorite Mark Twain quotes. It properly sets the tone: "In the first place, God made idiots. That was for practice. Then he made school boards."

I strongly believe that there are many great and qualified teachers who are dedicated to helping kids. My wife is one of them. But my experience with school boards is, well, like Mr. Twain said. I suspect you get my point of view. Especially when it comes to those that believe in the self-esteem-rooted, outcome-based education. Why? One of the very first casualties of the self-esteem culture is that of competition. Funny thing about competition, it wasn't too many years after studying it (academia is so quick to figure these things out) that most college professors realized that if we have any type of competition, in the end someone will win and someone will lose. Well, we can't have that now, can we? Losing is bad. It will make someone feel sad, depressed, or even downright unhappy. Any of those things could lead to poor self-esteem. Poor self-esteem will destroy a person. We must stop all competition.

Even grades in school are competitive and we just can't risk having one child do better than another. Grades should not be used either. After all, isn't that what tenure for college professors is all about? Once you are granted tenure, you are untouchable—free to pursue your academic goals without repercussion. There are a few problems with tenure, however. For starters, none of us in the real world have it. It only exists in the education arena. The rest of the world thrives on competition. Luckily, most schools don't buy into this concept. If the self-esteem Nazis had their way, that's how it would be.

We now have a global economy that is clearly based on the survival of the fittest. If self-esteem were the driving force in school, kids may make it through school being coddled and told that anything they do is fine, as long as it works for them. Then they hit the real world, only to be slapped hard across the face by reality as they transition to the work place.

Self-esteem extremists are not the only problem here. We as parents can also contribute to the self-esteem problem. Not that it's always a problem. To be more correct, it is the undeserved self-esteem that's the issue. How many of us were told by our parents that we could be or do anything we wanted? How many of us have told our own kids that same thing? Here's the catch . . . it's just not true! It may be alright when kids are young and need to open their minds to many possibilities. But not everyone can become anything. Eventually you need to help your children focus on the areas where they have an actual skill or aptitude. I had to face the fact that I was not going to be the world's best at everything . . . and maybe not at anything. But I could work and become my best at some things. It made sense to go with my strengths. That's what most of us do in the end. For example, my wife has a real gift for teaching kids. Tall ones, short ones, rich ones, poor ones, even very troubled ones. She's simply amazing as an elementary school teacher. That's why she became a school teacher—she's good at it. I could never do that. So, rather than force myself to become the best elementary school teacher I could be, I've chosen areas where, hopefully, I can excel. Well, this whole writing thing may not be a real skill, but I do like doing it. So indulge me a little. Okay, a lot.

The problem comes when some parents never help their kids face the reality that they have skills they should pursue and dreams that they may have to keep as dreams. Kids who are never told the truth actually have self-esteem based on false flattery. When the truth eventually hits them, they are devastated. I'm always amazed at the contestants on TV shows like *American Idol* that have dreams of being a pop star, but they are just plain horrible. Why didn't someone tell them that they really stink? The answer? No one wanted to hurt their self-esteem. They just wanted Simon Cowl to do it for them. How many parties, church socials, and other performances did these poor souls go through where everyone was embarrassed for them, but no one told them? Brutal, just brutal. They have spent so much time in an area where their chance of success is very slim and they often are just not prepared for their own future.

Not being prepared for the real world is only one concern. Again, let's turn to the Webster's definition of self-esteem: "a confidence and satisfaction in oneself."

Self-esteem is, by its definition, about me being happy with me. Here's the rub. To make sure I'm okay with me, I've got to focus on, well, ME. When I was young I used to go to an early morning Tae Kwon Do class at the local university. I have since determined that I'm nowhere near limber enough to continue that pursuit—tying my shoes is more strain than I care to admit. Anyway, on the wall in the fieldhouse where my class was held, there was a sign that displayed a quote by Confucius: "A man wrapped up in himself makes a very small bundle."

Now, this supposes that being a large bundle is better than being a small one. Were that statement about physical size, I'd have a problem with that. Actually, if being a large bundle from a body mass perspective was a good thing, I'd eat myself into a coma and gain superstar status in the process. But what our friend Confucius is talking about is not the physical but the inner self. Who we are, the positive influence we have, and the lives we touch. I've got to agree with him.

People who are self-centered (see definition above) are often shallow in the areas where real depth is required. The one relationship that self-esteem wants you to focus on is the one with yourself! You might notice from the chapter on happiness that *self* did not make the list of relationships that really matter. Why? Because when you focus on others you can't help but become affected.

Another old saying comes to mind: you can't help someone get to the top of the ladder without getting there yourself. There is a verse from the Bible that perhaps says it best: "For whosoever will save his life shall lose it: and whosoever will lose his life for my sake shall find it" (Matthew 16:25).

This may seem like a paradox. You save yourself and you are lost (sounds like self-esteem doesn't work here, does it?). You lose your life for his sake and you find your life—you will finally get what life is all about. If you study the scriptures further, it's pretty clear that when we "lose ourselves for Christ's sake," he's talking about helping others. His entire life and especially his death are all about that.

In my church, I have had the opportunity over the past few years to serve in a leadership role with a congregation that is composed entirely of single college students at the local university. Scary thought that I'd be allowed to work with impressionable minds, I know. One of the things I hear time and time again is that these students are very consumed with finding themselves. They want to be happy with who they are. My counsel is always the same. Focus on who you want to *become* and work on the attributes that will get you there. Don't focus on yourself, focus on others. Our self-esteem culture has made them believe that they just need to be happy with who they are; they need to turn inward—that whole small bundle thing. That is not what will bring happiness and peace.

Here's the problem. True self-respect does not come from negotiating with yourself or rationalizing away your shortcomings so you can feel good about who you are. If you've done something bad, you *should* feel bad. Not that you need to spend your life in misery, but remorse for things we've done wrong is a necessary step towards positive change. Life is *not* about just feeling complacent and comfortable with who you are. It is about growing, progressing, and becoming better tomorrow than you are today. That's not to say that you should be unhappy with yourself either. The key here is that your focus should not be yourself. When you turn outward instead of inward, your focus becomes helping others. And here's the amazing thing. When you help others become happy, you will discover that you have become very happy as well.

Your "self-esteem" will be strong, not because you talked yourself into it but because you have actual accomplishments in your life that warrant confidence. Not arrogance—confidence born of experience. Even failures give us experience and knowledge that help us do better the next time out.

So, there you have it. The only way to gain self-esteem is to not try to get self-esteem. In fact, what we really need to search for is what many would consider its opposite. I'm talking about *humility*.

Humility, or being humble, is too often associated with feeling bad about yourself—being brought to "the depths of humility." It can also be thought of as understanding your own insignificance in the universe. I've learned in church that being humble is a good thing. So, when I tried to apply either one of those definitions to my life, I discovered a few things. To begin with, both definitions make me think more about me, not less. The first definition made me miserable. Not a trait I was hoping to foster long-term.

Understanding my own nothingness actually has a useful part to it.

When I consider that I am only one person out of six billion or so that are on the earth at the moment, I begin to gain a new perspective on my relationship with God. I'm not only on a much lower rung than he is, I may not even be on the same ladder. The fact that God would pay attention to me or any of us at all brings a new sense of awe, respect, and deep gratitude. So that part is good. God is way up there, and I'm way, way down the totem pole—got it. But thinking about that any further can really make your head hurt.

What I have come to find out through a great deal of trial and error, with emphasis on the error, is that humility is the ultimate expression of turning outward and focusing on others. I mean real, genuine concern for someone besides myself, and I'm not talking about becoming a stalker here. Stalkers are all about themselves when you think about it, which I try not to do.

Humility is not having my own agenda at all, to the point that I'm willing to give up whatever is most precious to me for the sake of others— even (gulp) my own pride. In fact, true humility is only reached for each of us when we finally give ourselves over to what God wants us to do. I know, there's the religious part of me cropping up again. But I warned you right up front about that. Each one of us has something different that is most difficult to be willing to offer, but that is what is required. It takes a great deal of confidence to be willing to do that. That means helping someone else because they need help and because it's the right thing to do—not because I'm secretly thinking that helping them is going to help me in some way. Those who master humility aren't miserable, tortured souls. That would require thinking about themselves.

There are some great rewards in humility. As an example of one benefit, let's use an analogy . . . or is it an allegory, or a metaphor? Okay, let's use a *story* to illustrate a point here. Let's say you've been working for several years on a project that has become your life's work. You are scheduled to make a presentation on your project, which is the culminating event that will make your project complete. Everyone will be there, coworkers, peers, family, friends—everyone. The presentation is scheduled downtown at the nicest building in the city inside the auditorium.

You don't want to be late so you leave very early and drive yourself to the event. It's very crowded downtown and you can only find one parking spot. It's right in front of the building, but it's pretty small for your car. You drive around the block several times, but that spot is the only one. Still, you have plenty of time, and you know that if you make several small three-point turns you will eventually get your car into the spot. As you begin the maneuvers, you notice a bystander watching you. While you were just fine a moment ago, you begin to tense up. Now the person walks closer, staring at you through the windshield. Now you break a sweat. Before you know it, the bystander is laughing at you and heckling you from the sidewalk. You become so frustrated that you lose site of the goal of getting to your presentation and all you can think about is the heckler outside your window. That heckler, as it turns out, is you. Most of us are our own worst critics. That self-evaluation and ridicule we bring to ourselves often makes us lose sight of our ultimate goals. Humility removes the bystander from the equation, because it's not just about you anymore.

The biggest benefit of humility is that by being selfless and offering our free will, we gain confidence in ourselves. We know what we are doing is right. And that confidence leads to peace, which is the ultimate goal we are all after. (See the previous chapter—you aren't skipping around, are you?)

So there is the great paradox of this life. What we all really want is the long-term happiness that only comes through peace. Peace only comes through confidence, which only comes through humility, which only comes through not focusing on whether or not you are happy. Got it? Good. It took me a long time to figure all that out. And I'm still working on it every day. Still, another lesson learned.

Lesson 2

False self-esteem is bad. Self-esteem born of confidence from accomplishment is good. True humility through turning outward is the goal.

So what do I do about it?

Again, applying the lessons learned is what makes them useful. If a child learns that a fire is hot, but he still keeps putting his hand in the flames, did he really *learn* that fire is hot? My vote is no. Application of knowledge is proof that a lesson actually been learned. So here's what I try to do differently.

1. *Examine my motives.* We all have reasons for doing the things we do. We have our own bias and experience that influences our perception of a given situation. I find that when my motives for doing something are completely self serving, the outcome will not be good—even for me.

For example, I'm a sales and marketing guy at heart. I've discovered that the successes I have had in my business have not come from pursuing my *own* goals but by helping others meet their goals. I don't obtain success because I sell what I have to offer. I succeed because I help others meet their own needs. That's a huge difference. It forces me to change my approach and sometimes even my products to meet the needs of others. My motive should be to help clients, partners, and coworkers meet their objectives.

When my agenda clouds the picture, goals are not accomplished and my self-esteem suffers—and for good reason. As I set my agenda aside and help others meet their goals, then the humility I have shown in the process brings confidence and peace.

2. *Temper buying habits.* It's tough to find humility if I surround myself with the spoils of victory. I'm not suggesting that we shouldn't have a nice home, decent cars, and the like, but it's easy to cross the line. This is a hard one for me because, while I may not care about Rolex watches, I really love cars. I read car magazines, I surf car websites, and my wife will attest that I will notice a gorgeous car long before any attractive woman that may be driving it.

Going to the extremes in any one area of wants just makes it harder to focus on others and not on my own desires. In my case, the nicer the car, the smaller the bundle (back to Confucius again) I become.

3. *Inquire of others.* This behavior should go without saying, but it is rarely followed religiously. To become humble we need to set our agenda aside and focus on helping others. That becomes difficult to do if we don't know why others are doing what they are doing and what they are trying to accomplish. We need to continually ask questions and verify that we are still on the right track in helping others meet their objectives. It sounds so simple, but if adequate questioning is left out, there is no way to successfully help others.

Life's not always easy.
In fact that's rarely the case.
And to make it even tougher,
We often get lost in life's race.

We think we need to find ourselves,
Or just take time out for "me."
But have you ever seen that approach
Bring contentment, peace, or glee?

The truth is all too many people
Are concerned with self-esteem.
They focus on how they feel,
Rather than helping out the team.

Some turn their focus inward
To protect the image of him- or herself.
But the more effort given to personal wants,
The more happiness stays on the shelf.

We each have a different make up.
Each gene pool is unique.
But there are common things that push us all
Toward the inner peace we seek.

The key to our own personal quest
Causes many of us to stumble.
For the only way to reach the prize
Is through service that is humble.

So together we trudge though this life,
Helping others through heaven and hell.
And as we get lost in helping them,
We'll find we met our goal as well.

For no matter what the time period
In earth's history one may live,
Peace does not come from what we get;
It comes from what we give.

3

PRIDE

Pursuit 3

I wanted to protect my pride

This is the companion to lesson 2 on self-esteem. Since we ended that chapter talking about humility, pride is the next logical thing to discuss, largely because humility is really the only antidote to pride and is closely tied to self-esteem. We all seem to look for ways to be proud of ourselves and our accomplishments.

Not all forms of pride are bad, mind you. Some are quite good in fact. For example, civic pride is a positive thing. Pride in your country, your heritage, your children, and the accomplishments of another are all good—when kept in the proper perspective. In these instances, we actually use the word *pride* to mean grateful or thankful for, pleased with, or confident in. I'm okay with those definitions of pride. Most people believe that pride in your own accomplishments can even be alright if channeled correctly. I know I bought into that one for quite a while. Our own accomplishments can give us a confidence in ourselves to better ourselves, to take that next step into the unknown, right? As we discussed during our chat on self-esteem, confidence comes from experience and success, and through our relationship with others. Pride is not a help here. It is actually a hindrance. There are just too many pitfalls with pride to mess with it.

I was always told when I was young that if you were truly great at something, you had no need to boast of it; others would take care of that for you. Eventually, I learned that if you have truly rid yourself of pride, you don't need someone else to boast for you either. Seeking notoriety for your accomplishments in any form is prideful and not a desirable trait. So what's the big deal with pride anyway? Why is it so bad? There are plenty of reasons, so let's start at the top.

The most obvious problem with pride is that it usually makes you into a jerk. Selfishness has a way of doing that. Selfishness always accompanies pride—always. Think about it—do you like being with someone who is always prideful and thinking about himself? Of course you don't. I hate to break it to you, but if you are suffering from this all-too-common disease, people think you're a jerk too. Sorry, no loopholes on this one. You aren't so good that you are the only person to master the art of being prideful and self-centered and yet still charming and lovable. I know you think you've done that, but you haven't. That's the pride talking. Others see you for what you are—an arrogant, self-centered jerk.

Arrogance has another interesting side effect. It creates blind spots in your ability to evaluate your own behavior. Not a small little blind spot that you can compensate for by adjusting the rearview mirror. I'm talking about a huge gaping hole in your vision that makes you legally blind in the self-assessment category. If there were a driver's test for navigating through your life, your test results would have required you to be issued a white cane with a red tip, dark sunglasses, and a bus pass. Why? Because arrogance makes you unteachable. H. G. Wells said this about being willing to learn: "You have learned something. That always feels at first as if you had lost something."

What have you lost? A perception of something you thought was true, and now you know that you were not perfect, because you've gained new knowledge. Pride is much more comfortable than that. Why learn from your past if you already know it all? If someone else tries to offer a helpful critique, you quickly point out their mistakes and ignore their advice. After all, you're good, you're real good. I would go even further and say that arrogance makes you more than blind; it can make you stupid. When you can't see what is incredibly obvious to everyone else, what else do you call it? That's what I thought—stupid. Let me give you a real life example.

I've taught leadership and mentoring to corporate executives and consulted with people on these issues. I know—people paid me for advice—go figure. Not near enough pay, mind you. Was that my own pride talking? No, couldn't be—I've mastered that already. Anyway, I had someone with whom I worked closely who was a very bright person. I was having a very difficult time dealing with him because of his arrogance. This always led to friction with everyone in the company, and then there was his condescending tone.

To make a long story short, one day after teaching a leadership course, my arrogant associate and I got into a conversation about a real world issue that the course participants had brought with them to class. I explained in great detail a situation, including specifics of the conversation, results of the event—everything. The conversation ended with my associate shaking his head and saying, "Some people just don't get it, do they?" The problem was, the detailed description of the situation that I gave him was not from the class. It was an exact account of what had transpired between him and me just two days before. Blind and stupid.

Another pitfall of pride is an appetite that continually needs to be fed. C. S. Lewis put it this way: "Pride gets no pleasure out of having something, only out of having more of it than the next man."[1]

Pride is about comparisons. You never become happy with what you have or what you have accomplished because you always need to keep ahead of everyone else. Rather than being happy for another's success, you despise them for it. It's as though you are playing a zero sum game and if anyone else gets something, you are diminished. Even if another's success is not related to you or your world at all. And if they are in your field, your world, or your sphere, then the pain of their success is almost too much to bear. Pride brings a fear of losing that which we value most—the love and admiration of everyone we see. Of course, as we just talked about, if you are prideful, you don't have their love and admiration to begin with. You just think you do.

C. S. Lewis really knew a lot about this subject, and clearly he knew a great deal more than me, so forgive me for using just one more quote (at least in this chapter): "Pride can often be used to beat down the simpler vices. . . . Many a man has overcome cowardice, or lust, or ill-temper by learning to think that they are beneath his dignity—that is, by Pride. The devil laughs. He is perfectly content to see you become chaste and brave and self-controlled provided, all the time, he is setting up in you the Dictatorship of Pride. . . . For Pride is a spiritual cancer: it eats up the very possibility of love, or contentment, or even common sense."[2]

Wow. Read that again. We may actually use pride to get rid of other bad habits, all the while getting caught deeper in pride's snare. Let me explain it as follows. I'm not a lawyer, but my brother is. In addition to some really great lawyer jokes, I have actually learned a thing or two about the law. By the way, he no longer practices in a law firm, so his credibility is much higher than the typical lawyer. Anyway, in the United States, our legal system has two main categories of litigation. One is called civil litigation and the other is criminal litigation. The biggest difference between the two is that civil law is only concerned with an event that happened, without concern for the reasons it happened. Criminal law, on the other hand, not only deals with what happened, but also why it happened. It deals with *intent*. For example, killing someone is legal if it is in self-defense or the defense of another. Why does that matter to this conversation? As Lewis states, you can do the right things with the wrong intent and not benefit from the action. The intent of our actions *does* matter. God sees the intent, others usually see the intent, and no matter how much you deny it, if pride is your motivator, you'll eventually see it too. When that happens, lesson 3 is finally with your grasp.

Lesson 3

We don't need pride—period. Humility is much better.

So what do I do about it?

Applying this lesson is very similar to applying the lessons of self-esteem, but application here has more to do with self-evaluation.

1. *Do the right thing for the right reasons.* As part of my career, and in my church and social activities as well, I have to constantly ask myself why I'm doing what I'm doing. I constantly examine my intent. If I don't, often I will still choose a good thing to do, but I'll be doing it because I want to look good, or impress someone, or impress myself. In short, my pride looks for a feeding frenzy, and that is an appetite that can never be filled.

The amazing thing is, when I really do a good thing and my motive is not pride based, I always do it better. Without all the self-imposed pressure that pride brings, the quality of my work is higher, and I enjoy the experience much more.

2. *Never assume things are beneath you.* The older I get, the easier it is to think that I've earned the right to *not* do certain things. They're just beneath me. I live in a fast-paced, high-tech world. Yet, most Saturday

mornings, you can still see me mucking out our horses' stalls. Why, because I'm cheap? Well, yes . . . but I have five kids, remember? I could certainly guilt/threaten one of them into doing it. The truth is, it's good for me. It's a lowly act for our horses and for my wife, because she'd go do it if I didn't. Women. Can't live with 'em, can't let 'em throw out their backs shoveling manure. Stall mucking reminds me of the stuff I had to do as a child; it keeps me grounded. And when I push my pride aside, why shouldn't I do it? I get good exercise and it provides quiet reflection time—just me and the manure. Plus, it's hard to feel prideful when you look and smell the way I do at the end of that weekly adventure!

3. *Do as you'd have done unto you.* If pride has been your constant companion for quite some time, it gets hard to step back and evaluate your motives. A good way for me to do this is to put myself in the spectator role and imagine someone else behaving the way I do. What would I think about *their* behavior? Prideful people are really good at seeing the flaws of others. When you put yourself in a role reversal like that, it can really be an eye opener.

To put it another way . . .

I try to go through life
With my conscience as my guide.
That usually works quite well,
Unless it's dulled with a sense of pride.

At first it seemed so innocent
To take pride in what I do.
And then before I knew it,
I needed to do it better than you.

I fretted about what others do
And how that reflected on me.
I was blinded by my own desire
To do things perfectly.

I finally had to face the fact
That applause was what I craved.
Even though my acts were good,
My motives were depraved.

Finally, in deep despair,
For happiness could not be found,
I saw myself as others did,
And in shame I nearly drowned.

With a real deep breath I did my best
To right the wrongs I'd done.
I no longer tried at any cost
To be declared the number one.

Instead, I help those I meet
To do the best they can do.
The more I focus on their success,
The happier I become too.

Admitting the truth was hard to do,
But it could no longer be denied.
I had finally felt I was truly alive
Through the death of my own pride.

Notes
1. C. S. Lewis, *Mere Christianity*, 122.
2. Ibid., 125.

4

FREEDOM

Pursuit 4

I longed for freedom

I remember when I was a teenager and just couldn't wait to get out and on my own. Doing what I wanted, when I wanted: that was my dream. No more chores (yes, they were called chores, even though we didn't live near a farm). No more controlling my TV time. I could watch reruns of *Gilligan's Island* all day if I wanted. No more curfews set by my parents. My dad was a stickler on this one. He actually expected me to be home when he told me to be home. The few times I missed my curfew, even if only by a minute or two, I was in big trouble. From being grounded to losing one privilege or another, the results were swift and sure. Talk about cruel and unusual punishment.

My little sister had it better than me. By her turn to be a teenager, Mom and Dad were worn down. She's never properly thanked me for that. But I'm still willing to accept cash anytime she feels the guilt of a debt unpaid. Anyway, my sister could actually sneak in quietly, turn back the clock on my parents' nightstand, wake them to let them know she was home, and then reset the clock after they had fallen asleep. No doubt about it, she was good. In my day, Dad would have heard me do that. Yes, sir, freedom was the dream of my youth. I see that same gleam in my own kids' eyes from time to time. Though they get away with more than I did at their age, I'm afraid. But that's another story.

Eventually, the time came. Mom and Dad no longer controlled my day. In fact, they went from making sure I didn't spend too much time with any one girl to urging me to find the right girl and settle down. Go figure . . . they didn't want to control my every movement after all. I was on my own, free to do what I wanted with my life. Still, my parents have always been there to give advice and guidance when asked, but they've been careful to never butt in of their own accord. Now that some of my kids are getting to that age, I can see how difficult that must have been for them. I'd actually like small chips implanted in my kids' brains that would allow my wife and me to plant the proper suggestions at the proper time. Not total mind control, mind you, just the big things. You know, who to marry, career path, naming their kids after me, stuff like that. But I digress. The point is, freedom is the right of every person. There is a catch, however. There is no way to have freedom without dealing with the consequences of our freedom. We have the freedom to choose, but we must also live with the choices we have made and the results they bring. A lot of people seem to have a problem with that fact.

One group of people that doesn't seem to deal well with freedom are those that are in the *victim* category. Being a victim is great. If you are a victim, nothing is your fault. Someone else did something to you, and you did nothing wrong in the process. While that may be true for victims of crime, it holds little water for victims of life. But what about the bad things people did to your ancestors generations ago? Lawsuits for *reciprocity?* That must be worth some big money! Please. Bad stuff can and does happen in life. That's when our freedom matters most. Let me give you a few examples of what I mean.

The first is an example from my own life. I started my first software company when I was twenty-three years old and still in college. We had grown to thirty employees or so and were expanding into some exciting areas. I had brought on investors along the way to help fund the development of our cutting-edge technologies. To make a long story short, the investors did not do everything they said they would do, and in fact, decided they wanted my technology for one of their other companies. The bottom line was that they were in a position to take the company down, take the software they wanted, and fold it into a company of which they had full control. I was robbed! I was the victim, right? Well, the truth is, I made decisions along the way that allowed my company to become vulnerable. While the investors did not live up to their word, I was not without fault. In the end, I had lost my dream and was devastated. It took a while for me to realize that my company had died, but I hadn't. That was one of those pivotal moments in my life. My father sat me down and said, among other things, one statement that I will never forget: "It doesn't matter what happens to you; it's how you handle what happens to you that matters."

That hit me like a ton of bricks. I realized that I had the freedom to choose where I went from there. I was no longer a victim. As I watch the victims in the world around me, I'm amazed at the effort that is spent on ensuring that they can stay victims. Even if you find yourself in the position of having done nothing wrong and others have truly wronged you, the freedom is there for you to choose to move forward and do the best you can from that time on. You can lament over the wrongs that have happened to you and you can try to get as many people as possible on your side. You may feel more justified in your position by doing so, but has it done anything to help you get where you want to be? No. Rationalization and justification are some of the best tools you will ever find to ensure you are not successful.

Another example of being a victim is one that is much more subtle. I grew up near a family that started with very little, but the father founded and grew a very successful company. The oldest son in that family was a friend of mine. When most of us went off to college, my friend went to work in the family business. His father begged him to go to college and get the business education he would need to take over the company someday. The company would even pay him handsomely to do so. But the full-time money was too good, and the studies in school were too hard. My friend simply didn't want to put in the effort.

As time went on, the father tried to let his son take over. Smart though he was, my friend lacked the skills to run the organization, things didn't work out, and the company was in trouble. He was upset when his father took control of the company again and he decided to leave, only to find that no one wanted to hire an uneducated person with experience in only one company. He was faced with the direct results of exercising his freedom to choose. A victim of his own choices, he chose to use blame as his justification. Blame is a great tool for victims.

Another problem many people face when wanting their freedom is the feeling of *entitlement*. The concept of freedom flies right in the face of those who feel entitled to certain things in their lives. Freedom gives you the freedom to succeed, but it also gives you the freedom to fail. Entitlement seekers don't grasp that last part. In the United States today, we have an ever-growing number of people who claim they love freedom but don't understand that the freedom our founding fathers envisioned is the freedom of opportunity, not the guarantee of success. As a result, successful people and companies are vilified. Surely they exploited those that are less fortunate than they are. They must have done something evil to have accomplished so much.

While there may be a small few that have taken advantage of others, in most cases, what they exploited was their own opportunities, intelligence, hard work, and probably some favorable timing. Does that make them evil? Shouldn't they be taxed and forced to share their ill-gotten gains with those they must have oppressed along the way? There are many who feel that way. The true underpinnings of freedom are lost on them. Mark Twain puts it best: "Don't go around saying the world owes you a living. The world owes you nothing. It was here first."

Once I was out of high school and on my own, I quickly discovered a few things. I was free to play all the time, and my professors would then be free to fail me. If I focused on school, I was still free to choose any major I wanted—even one that would not give me the skills necessary to get a job. Early in my college years, I married a wonderful woman and we had a great time together—and we still do. While we were free to do as we pleased, we quickly found ourselves doing all that boring stuff our parents were doing—working, cleaning, studying, and so forth. We found that all this freedom brought with it a great deal of responsibility. And here's the crazy thing: we didn't mind! Personally, I liked doing my part to contribute to my family and to society.

Freedom had brought me a new sense of duty and honor. As a newlywed, I actually cleaned our apartment without being asked. That never happened in my bedroom as a kid. My mom would have to get after me and ultimately threaten some unspeakable punishment, like not going to play with my friends, before I would give in. But now, if I didn't do my part, my wife would have to do it all. That didn't seem right. How long could she love and respect a slug that didn't do anything? While I was always free to choose, I found that I chose to do what I *needed* to do, not always just what I *wanted* to do. I chose duty over self. Who saw that coming? I would never have believed it when I was a teenager (I'm sure my parents would concur on that one). And what's more, I liked it. I felt a sense of accomplishment and confidence. I had actually *earned* self-esteem. There was no taking time just for me so I could "find myself" and feel good about me. I did feel good about myself, but it was based on accomplishment, not selfish rationalization.

As a teenager, I craved freedom, but with freedom I found that fulfilling my duty was what I really wanted. As it turns out, all great people throughout history figured out the same thing. Not that I'm in their same class, mind you. But it's nice to know I've figured a few things out correctly along the way. One of the best examples of duty is the true story of a man named Abraham Davenport. His story used to be told quite often in the United States. Abraham was a Puritan from Connecticut and a leader during the Revolutionary period of our nation's history. There was an event that became known as The Dark Day. It happened in May of 1780. The skies over New England were unusually dark. Some speculate that forest fires combined with odd weather and a solar eclipse could have been the cause, but I don't think anyone knows what really happened. Today, many would attribute it all to global warming, to be sure. Rock and roll stars would have done a Puritan Aid concert had they been alive at the time. Anyway, on that day, the Connecticut General Assembly was in session in Hartford. As the world outside grew dark, so did the inside of the chamber where the politicians had gathered. Panic set in. People believed the end of the world had come. Here is how the poet John Greenleaf Whittier told what happened that day:

> There fell over the bloom and sweet life of the Spring
> Over the fresh earth and the haven of noon,
> A horror of great darkness, like the night
> In day of which the Norland sagas tell,
> The Twilight of the Gods. The low-hung sky
> Was black with ominous clouds, save where its rim
> Was fringed with a dull glow, like that which climbs
> The crater's sides from the red hell below.
> Birds ceased to sing, and all the barnyard fowls
> Roosted; the cattle at the pasture bars
> Lowed, and looked homeward; bats on leathern wings
> Flitted abroad; the sounds of labor died;
> Men prayed, and women wept; all ears grew sharp
> To hear the doom-blast of the trumpet shatter
> The black sky, that the dreadful face of Christ
> Might look from the rent clouds, not as he looked
> A loving guest at Bethany, but stern
> As Justice and inexorable Law.
> Meanwhile in the old State House, dim as ghosts
> Sat the lawgivers of Connecticut,
> Trembling beneath their legislative robes.
> "It is the Lord's Great Day! Let us adjourn,"

Some said; and then, as if with one accord,
All eyes were turned to Abraham Davenport.
He rose, slow cleaving with his steady voice
The intolerable hush. "This well may be
The Day of Judgment which the world awaits;
But be it so or not, I only know
My present duty, and my Lord's command
To occupy till he come. So at the post
Where he hast set me in his providence
I choose, for one, to meet him face to face,
No faithless servant frightened from my task,
But ready when the Lord of the harvest calls;
And therefore, with all reverence, I would say,
"Let God do his work, we will see to ours.
Bring in the candles." And they brought them in.

Now there was a man who understood life. Work is good and honorable and if it was to be the end of the world, what better place to be found than doing your duty? Robert E. Lee wrote to his son while he was away at school of that event which had happened so many years before. He said: "There was quietness in that man's mind, the quietness of heavenly wisdom and inflexible willingness to obey present duty. Duty, then, is the sublimest word in our language. Do your duty in all things like the old Puritan. You cannot do more, you should never wish to do less."

I don't know if duty ranks quite that high on my list. But from a General's point of view, you can see why he would think so. True freedom brings a sense of responsibility and duty.

Lesson 4

With freedom comes responsibility. Duty is a privilege freedom provides.

So what do I do about it?

1. *Be anxiously engaged.* By that, I mean get involved. And get involved in more than one area of life. I have a friend and neighbor who is a great

example of this one. He has a very demanding and interesting job that could easily swallow up all of his energy, should he let it. Still, he is active is his church and has held many ecclesiastical positions of authority over the years. But he does not stop there. He is a district chair for his political party and often serves as a state delegate, which requires attending conventions and other political functions. Were that not enough, this past year he served in a volunteer role as president of the annual Fourth of July festival that we have in our area. It is actually the largest Independence Day celebration in the entire country. Heading up the festival is a huge undertaking, to say the least. On top of all that, he's an attentive husband and father. Is he an overachiever? I don't think so. He's a man who appreciates the freedoms he has to the point that he sees serving others as his duty.

2. *Be responsible for your actions.* Those with a strong sense of gratitude for their freedom also feel a sense of responsibility and duty. Those traits translate into personal responsibility, drive, and ambition. Let's face it—life is not fair. But it is our duty to do our part the best we can. I learned that in business, as I mentioned early in the chapter, but it took a while to translate that into all aspects of my life. And frankly, I'm still not there. But it's my duty to keep trying, progressing, and doing the best that I can. It's a daily struggle to ensure that I meet the obligations and opportunities that lie before me.

3. *Look forward not back.* Duty is not about resting on your laurels or making sure you get the proper credit for your actions. People driven by duty are so busy doing all they can in the present and planning for the future that they don't have time to look back. They do take the lessons they've learned with them as they move forward, but the key is, they keep moving. Duty does not involve self-justification, blame, or vindication of past actions. Those things do not help accomplish the tasks ahead.

To put it another way . . .

Of all the rights that we hold dear,
Our founding fathers give just three.
Pursuing happiness, sustaining life,
And that of our liberty.

The last one is perhaps the best
And most important right of all.

Without it happiness can't be found
As life is driven by freedom's call.

We are free to go throughout our lives
And pursue what we love most.
We are also free to just sit back,
And through our lives, just coast.

But liberty has its strings attached
And dues that must be paid.
With freedom to choose the path we take
Come consequences we can't evade.

The key to freedom and liberty
Is to use its power well.
Through honor, duty, and hard work,
Freedom's sweetness we may smell.

Equality of opportunity
Is what freedom lovers crave.
Equality of outcome
Is only sought by those less brave.

With freedom comes the chance to win,
And also the chance to lose.
But things in life worth having
Are worth the risk and work we choose.

For happiness is not an entitlement
It's a goal we have the right to pursue.
Only by using our freedom well
Will happiness find me or you.

5

CONTROL

Pursuit 5

I wanted control of my life

I've been an *entremanure* (that's an entrepreneur, but you realize how full of it you are at times) for nearly all of my adult life. I started my first real company at the age of twenty-three. I used to joke that I had to start my own business because no one would hire me. Nobody laughed—but that's another story. The truth was, I could get a job back then, but I saw an opportunity and I went for it.

A side bar—once you've ventured off on your own, you eventually get to the point where it is very difficult to find a job if you want to work for someone else. Not that you aren't able to adjust; it's that other employers think you won't be able to adjust. They believe that you will either try to take things over in their company or you'll get frustrated and strike out on your own again. That's typically not true. If a former entrepreneur wants to work for someone else, it's often because they've learned that being a business owner wasn't for them. As a business owner you have to deal with a lot of things that you never thought about much—employee issues, benefits, regulations, and so forth, and you don't get to do much of what you started the business for in the first place. If that's not their reason, they've likely been beat up enough from the experience that the ownership bug is completely out of their system. So if you come across one of these poor souls looking for work, don't disqualify them because you think they have to be king. Enough said.

For me, I've always liked having something to do that at least had the chance of a big payoff down the road. Not necessarily in money, though I'm not opposed to that. Okay, I'd probably even like that. But

I've dreamed of really being able to set my own schedule and doing what I enjoy. Control of my life has been the goal. Plus, I've always had a low threshold for incompetence, or at least my view of incompetence. Things get done my way when I'm the boss because I'm the one in control, right? Control, control, control . . . that's what I've always wanted.

Funny, it's never really worked that way. For starters, there are those other things you have to deal with. You know—people. Other people. Many of them want things their own way too. So how do you get your own way and have them get their own way? Most control-loving people try to convince everyone else that their way is *the* way. Then the world will conform to them and all will be right in the universe once again. Nope, that's the wrong answer, simply because it just doesn't work, at least not for long. I learned after a few mishaps in managing employees that you don't manage employees. You can manage stuff or processes but not people. In business you need to lead people. And leaders are people that other people *choose* to follow. It's not a control thing. When people have the right tools, vision, and support, they tend do to the right thing. Sorry, that's the leadership consultant coming out in me. Please pardon my rambling. I almost went into a trance and used words like envision, empower, and inspire. The shock of those things popping into my head stunned me back to reality. Whew! That was a close one.

Of course, not all people are control mongers. They just see things based on their own experience, as we all do. That often leads them to do things differently. I finally learned to give people in my employ goals and certain boundaries, but laying out the details of exactly how to meet those goals I left to them. Micromanaging shows a lack of trust and an over abundance of ego. Everyone needs to feel a sense of accomplishment. If I controlled everything, my employees felt no sense of achievement—no earned self-worth. And the job typically does not get done as well when someone's heart is not in it.

So besides people, I've found other problems with control. The biggest one was hard to admit, because it was and still is, well . . . me. Eventually I had to admit that no matter how good I think I am at something, I'm not perfect. Not even close. There are always other ways, often better ways, to do things than *my* way. For a control freak, that's difficult to digest. Imagine other people using their own skills, experience, and intellect to do something better than I would have done it. Who knew? Truthfully, probably everyone but me. There you have it from a recovering control addict.

Hi, my name is Barry, and I'm a controlaholic. Life has its own twelve-step program to help get over this one. Reality will usually seep in for all but the most stubborn of us. Hopefully I've learned from my mistakes.

So how did I get to be such a control monger in the first place? I suppose it really hit a fever pitch for me when I started running my own business. Some people start small companies and slowly grow them. But most of my businesses have been in the high tech world where things would move very quickly, and my goals would move even faster. That translates into taking risk, lots of risk. More risk than I should have ever taken, that's for sure. I've found you need more control when you are in deep, at risk, or in trouble. Everything must go a certain way or your world collapses around you. And you often need things to happen quickly, before your tenuous situation is exposed and everything comes down like a house of cards. A wise man once told me that you should never negotiate anything when you really need it to happen. You tend to accept terms that you wouldn't if you had many options to choose from. But, in start up mode, the "any port in a storm" mentality can become the rule rather than the exception. All of a sudden you have investors, employees, and clients all with great demands. If everything doesn't go just right, well . . . you get the picture. That's my excuse and I'm sticking to it. Anyway, trying to control everything is simply not possible.

So if controlling everything in life is not possible, and really not even desirable, what do we do? For the answer to this, I pulled from my consulting/training background, as well as advice from someone much wiser than me.

First is a concept from the business side. One of the things I've helped companies with was change management. Without getting into boring details (trust me, there are *lots* of boring details), there was one thing that we would always drill into a client's brain. That is, "change is not a single event, it is a continual process." When you apply that to your personal life, it means that the only thing that is constant is change. It always happens. So rather than deal with each thing that goes differently than you expect as a major crisis, expect it and accept it. That's not to say you have to love and embrace every unexpected thing in your life, but you do need to develop the skills and the attitude to handle deviations from your grand plan. I'm a big football fan, and there is an analogy that is useful from watching a game. My favorite players are the ones who handle themselves with dignity. While a ridiculous end zone dance is fairly common, I like the guys who simply put the ball down or hand it to the referee and trot off the field instead—like they've been there many times before and expect to be there again. They are still happy with the touchdown; they just seem to deal with their good fortune in a better way. The same holds true for a mistake on the field. Rather than beating themselves up, they shake off what they can't change and focus on doing better the next time. If you handle yourself similarly, you'll get less stressed when things don't go your way and you'll be more gracious when they do. Plus, the attitude of expecting change will allow you to identify good or bad changes sooner, because you are trained to look for them. The sooner you see them, the sooner you can act to avoid downsides or take advantage of the good things that come your way.

This leads me to the second concept that took me a while to really understand—serendipity. We've all heard the word, but most people don't fully understand what it means and how it can affect your life. I've got to give credit to a wise man and best-selling author named Richard Eyre who helped me with some of the concepts here. I hope my mentioning him doesn't tarnish his reputation . . . but I warned him and he didn't seem to mind. Anyway, most of you probably think that the term *serendipity* means to find some good thing that you weren't really looking for. That's true, but it's only part of the meaning.

The word *serendipity* was first coined by Horace Walpole (1717–1797), fourth Earl of Orford, son of Prime Minister Robert Walpole, connoisseur, antiquarian, and author of the famous Gothic novel, *The Castle of Otranto* (London, 1765). The term comes from an old story called "The Three Princes of Serendip."

Serendip was the ancient Arab name for an island that is widely believed to be the current country of Sri Lanka. The actual story was first published in Venice in 1557. The story opens with the following lines: "In ancient times there existed in the country of Serendippo, in the Far East, a great and powerful king by the name of Giaffer. He had three sons who were very dear to him. And being a good father and very concerned about their education, he decided that he had to leave them endowed not only with great power, but also with all kinds of virtues of which princes are particularly in need."

The story moves on to the sons having many great adventures and using abductive reasoning skills. For the record, abductive reasoning skills are sort of the inverse of deductive reasoning skills, because you see the evidence before you know there is an issue to be dealt with. As their wisdom grew, the princes would keep discovering good things during their journeys to fulfill one quest or another, things that they were not actually looking for, by being aware of everything around them.

The most known example from the *Three Princes* story is when the princes were traveling on a quest in a foreign land. They eventually came across a man looking for a camel. They asked him if the camel was blind in one eye, missing a tooth, and lame. The camel driver said yes, and they told him the direction it had headed. The man still could not find the camel and caught up to the three princes again. This time they told him the camel was carrying a pregnant woman with a load of butter on one side and honey on the other. Their account was not only correct, but so detailed the camel driver became convinced the three young men had stolen his camel.

They were taken captive and brought before the ruler of the land, Emperor Behram. As they recounted their story, the princes admitted that they had never actually seen the camel but had pieced together clues to ascertain the facts of the situation. Shortly thereafter, the camel was found and the three young men were proved innocent. The emperor was so impressed with their reasoning skills, he asked them how they figured out all the details. Along their journey, they noticed things along their path, such as the way the grass was eaten only on the left side of the road, even though the grass on the right side of the road was better. That led them to believe the camel was blind in the right eye. They found bits of grass along the road that had fallen from the camel's mouth of the size that would indicate a missing tooth. The drag in the footprints on the road pointed to the camel being lame. On one side of the road they noticed ants covering drips of something and flies attracted to drips on the other side. Ants love butter and flies love honey. At one point, they noticed a woman's footprints leading off to the side of the road and handprints on the ground where, in her heavy state, she had used them to push her to her feet again after finishing her "business." That led to her being a pregnant woman.

None of these things really mattered to them at the time they observed them and were not the focus of their quest. When they were finally told of the missing camel, they were able to piece together all the things they had seen. The serendipitous part came later when Emperor Behram showered them with gifts and made them his advisors. The princes were not looking for these gifts, but their cleverness, wisdom, and keen observation skills made it possible.

Many of our scientific discoveries have come about through serendipity as well. Archimedes's principle of buoyancy and water displacement was discovered while Archimedes was taking a bath and noticed the water in the tub rising as he submerged his body. He became so excited when the concept hit him that he jumped out of the tub and ran naked down the street yelling, "Eureka!" (I found it!). I hope if I ever have that great of an idea that I'm not in the bathtub at the time. I'd like to spare my neighbors from that experience.

Walpole's original definition of the word *serendipity*, when discussing the three princes, was, "They were always making discoveries, by accident and sagacity, of things they were not in quest of."

As Walpole's writings and others' on the subject portray, there are a few key elements that today's more vague definition does not include. First is the idea of "sagacity," which means in a state of being sagacious. Not real helpful yet? By turning to the Webster's definition, there is finally some insight on what this word really means: "keen and farsighted penetration and judgment."

Serendipity is not about stumbling onto good fortune brought on by dumb luck. You have to be *sagacious*. Luck is really not a key element here. The main thing is to be aware of what is going on around you and taking advantage of events and information that are in your path. In truth, serendipity is in all of our paths if we are perceptive enough to see what is there.

The other element of serendipity is that the princes did not gain their knowledge by sitting at home in Dad's castle and watching the plasma screen on the wall. They were constantly on quests. They were actively pursuing worthwhile goals.

Combining worthy pursuits with a keen sense of discernment brings about or *causes* serendipity. It's not just happenstance. These two elements in play bring about a state of mind where a person's own awareness allows him to find something better than what he was looking for, a good thing he could not have planned but was aware enough to notice.

My personal belief is that God is a big fan of this type of serendipity. He places things in all of our lives that we have to find while in pursuit of good things. We have to be engaged in good works and aware of what is around us. Only then can we take advantage of the blessings he'd like us all to have. It's a pretty slick way of doing things from his perspective. We all have equal opportunity, but only those on the right path recognize the gifts for what they are.

In my own life, I discovered while trying to build my first company just how important my family was. I was so focused on the business (my quest) I thought about little else. As things took a down turn, eventually my company was gone. On my first day at home with no business to go to, my wife simply asked what was next and what she could do to help. No one else was there for me. The rats had already jumped from my sinking ship. I learned a lesson that I had long needed to learn, but I wasn't looking for. It's been one of the best lessons of my life: what really matters most—family.

Now I approach my work life differently and have a deep appreciation for my family that I never had before. While some may argue that I had no place to go but up, I know the lesson taught to me by my wife, lessons I wasn't looking for, made me a better father and husband. This is similar to the logic Christ used in the Bible when he spoke in parables. To some the parables are nothing more than stories or fables. But to those that are in tune with God, they teach vital truths and provide guidance on many levels and much deeper meaning. Serendipity works the same way. The more we learn to take advantage of those "discoveries or accidents that we are not in quest of" as Walpole would say, the more we hone our skill to find more discoveries or accidents that we can take advantage of.

Only a control freak would have put this much effort into determining why the whole control thing just doesn't work. As it turns out, I didn't even have to rationalize on this one. Control is highly overrated. Being able to be aware, adapt, and appreciate the changes that come my way is much more satisfying than getting exactly what I thought I wanted. But don't tell my family. I'm still trying to milk the control thing when it suits me. So, after being clubbed in the head by life a few times, I finally learned lesson 5.

Lesson 5

Total control of one's life is neither possible, nor desirable. The key is to be aware of what is around you and take advantage of the good things in your path that may be unexpected.

So what do I do about it?

1. *Have an attitude of gratitude.* At the very least, I try not to get frustrated when things don't go exactly as I would like them to. As each

deviation from my grand plan comes about, I try to look at them more objectively. What can I learn from them? Is there something I need to change? Maybe there is a problem lurking that I can be more proactive about resolving, or maybe there is an unexpected opportunity that I can take advantage of—even if it wasn't in the plan from the beginning. Having a better attitude about the unexpected things that come our way will, in itself, help to bring about serendipitous good fortune.

2. *Keep a sharp eye*. Remember, we all need to be more sagacious. That means we have to pay more attention to the world around us and look for things that might be opportunities or pitfalls. Sometimes we can become too focused on the tasks at hand and we miss things. I've always been amazed that truly great people seem to find the time to read on a variety of subjects. They are also involved in many facets of life, not just one primary thing. I finally realized that doing all those things keeps their minds open and increases their opportunities. They are being sagacious! At times I have to force myself out of my one-track mind and take a look around. Life is more rich and full when it is not one dimensional.

3. *Plan for change*. So how do I do that? Well, to start with, I have to plan, not just stumble around in the dark hoping lady luck will find me. Remember, the princes were always going about doing good things. Planning is more than a to-do list. Good plans include planned evaluations where you are forced to step back and take a look around. They should also include mechanisms that are already in place to handle disputes or unexpected events.

For example, if you are planning to move your business to a new building, your plan should first start with a setting criteria for how to select a new location—before you even have options to choose from. You might want a committee that can help with the evaluation of each location, and you may want to decide ahead of time how you will handle disputes if they can't agree. You also need a way to deal with last-minute changes or new information that comes your way. Good planning will help you identify opportunities sooner because you already know the criteria that will help reach your goals. You will also be able to see problems sooner and deal with them more effectively before they get out of hand.

To put it another way . . .

My way or the highway—
An all too common phrase

Used by way too many of us
As we navigate life's maze.

But our way is not the only way.
It's just the one that we know best.
We may like another's path
If we'd put it to the test.

Though we all like to be in control
And avoid experimenting with the unknown.
If Edison and Bell had felt that way,
We'd be in the dark, without a phone.

Being in control has its faults,
Especially from another's point of view.
When control is dictated by just one,
Satisfaction is found by few.

When total control is the goal,
The outcome may not be in doubt.
But the end result is never better
Than what you had planned out.

The only thing constant in this life
Is that the unexpected does arise.
Managing such change is a vital skill
Because total control never really applies.

Besides the fact that control is a myth,
It's not what we should even desire.
It prevents good things from coming our way
Beyond what we alone could conspire.

Serendipity is much better than control;
It's the good things for which we don't plan.
By being aware of things placed in our path
And by serving our fellow man.

6

TOLERANCE

Pursuit 6

I wanted to be tolerant of others

My generation is different than the one before—especially in the tolerance category. In my parents' generation, interracial dating and marriage were very rare. My parents were certainly not in favor of it when I was growing up. In my generation, it's much more accepted. We've come a long way. When I was young, I really wanted to be more tolerant than others I had seen. I still think if you marry someone from a different culture you will have a lot of challenges, but that's because you'll see the world differently in so many ways. It has nothing to do with race or intolerance, just with difference.

Did I mention that people are and can be different from each other? That's okay, really. For example, men are different from women and vice versa. They just are. No matter how much one group or another tries to blur the lines, it will always be that way. Like when my wife and I had our first two kids. Our oldest is a boy. From the moment he could indicate a preference, he chose cars, trucks, and balls. He's still a sports nut to this day. He liked the typical guy stuff right off. We didn't push him that way; he just chose that way. My daughter, on the other hand, seemed to favor girl stuff as a general rule. My other kids have followed suit based on gender as well. Not that there haven't been a few exceptions to that rule . . . like the times my son played with my daughter's big pink Barbie limo. But at least it was a car—a big car. It's a guy thing. Anyway, tolerance is the issue, not differences. I just wanted to point out that differences are okay. Did I make that point? I hope so. Those who think we can't be different tend to be socialists, fascists, communists, or Nazis. Not a crowd

I'd like to hang out with. So let's move on to the subject at hand.

Tolerance—what a concept. Who could ever be against that? It's such a nice, kind, benevolent word. I mean, can't we all just get along? No one wants to be labeled as intolerant. Or worse yet, a bigot. And truthfully, in society today there is less intolerance than at any time in the history of the planet. That's all good, right? Well, in some aspects it's a good thing. For example, anyone from any racial background can be a success, if they are willing. And I mean IF they are willing to work, with no excuses. There are countless examples of success for all races and both genders. There still are only *two* genders, technically at least, though I must admit despite my rant in the previous paragraph, there are several shades of gray on this one. In all walks of life there are people who have risen above all odds and realized their dreams. The oppression argument simply does not hold water (see my victim rant in the freedom chapter). But there are still those who are convinced everything bad that happens is a grand conspiracy to keep them down. The truth is, the only thing that holds these people back is their own attitude. There are still rules to success, including hard work and persistence, but the possibilities are out there. Society's push for tolerance has helped bring that about. That's a good thing. So why am I about to take a different stance on tolerance? There are a lot of reasons. I'll take on the big ones one at a time.

In our culture, there is perhaps no other subject that has been more abused than tolerance. How could that possibly happen? Interestingly enough, the biggest abusers are those who are screaming for tolerance. Back when the civil rights movement took hold in the United States in the 1960s, there were some very legitimate concerns. Martin Luther King Jr. really had the right idea. He wanted people to be judged not for the color of their skin but for the content of their character. While things are not perfect these days and racial divides do still exist, thanks to King and others, things have gotten a lot better. So much so that today's so-called civil rights leaders don't have nearly the influence that they once did. But that's because they've actually gotten a lot of what they wanted! Or at least what the people wanted. But leaders like Jesse Jackson and Louis Farrakhan don't keep their power by helping others to become empowered. They *need* people to feel like they are victims. As a result they say outlandish things and extort money (money = power, Politics 101) by threatening boycotts and protests in a desperate attempt to stay relevant. The more they use these tactics, the less effective they become. Gratefully, they don't seem to know how to write a new playbook. They become more obscure the more they try to get attention.

One of the unspoken truths is that people who want tolerance do not really want tolerance. They may start out that way, but they quickly move from wanting tolerance to wanting acceptance, then endorsement, and finally domination. Take the gay community for example. In the beginning of the "gay movement" they just wanted to be left alone and not beat up or killed. I can understand and even agree with that concept. But they quickly moved to wanting acceptance and endorsement. Today, they put forth the ultimate goal, that of having a legal marriage. Please. A marriage is between a man and a woman and always has been. It was Adam and Eve, not Adam and Steve. Who set that up? Just God. If you don't like it, take it up with him. But gays want to pretend that they are mainstream, even more mainstream than the heterosexual crowd. One of the key elements of a marriage is to raise children. Countless studies and common sense tell us that kids do MUCH better when they have the influence of a father and mother. That's just the plain truth. Doing something that is wrong, and then doing it a lot and getting others to do it does not make it right. The truth is, most people are not comfortable with homosexuality, either for religious reasons, practical reasons, or just because it's creepy. Personally, I fall into all three categories. That doesn't mean that we (we being all straight people) won't tolerate gays. Most of us don't care if they have civil unions of some sort. But marriage? That's ours and you can't have it. It would just demean something that we hold dear, even sacred.

The liberal political movement is much the same way. Whenever a conservative position is expressed, liberals claim a lack of tolerance. The truth is that a point of view that is different from theirs has been expressed. The real intolerance is on their part for not allowing for a different point of view. Diversity is only achieved when the world sees things the liberal way, even when the overwhelming majority disagrees with their position. I'm not completely blind on this subject. I realize that conservatives can be, and often are, guilty of this as well. But for liberals, it's an art form.

So why doesn't the vast majority speak out? It's because political correctness (PC) doesn't allow us to. Our society has actually gotten to the point where extremists on any point of view are emboldened and even receive preferential treatment above the regular people. While we may in theory have freedom of speech, it is limited for regular folks. The extremists are the ones who can really exercise that freedom. The preferential treatment comes in many ways. Sometimes it is in the things they can say, but it is also in the way they can behave. I'll give you an example from my own experience. This has to do with the gay community again. I'm not trying to single them out, but this story makes a good point.

A few years ago I had an exhibit at a trade show in Orlando. My wife consented to come to the show and help work our exhibit. She and I arrived a few days early so we could do the Disney experience. As we went into the park, I noticed that most people were wearing red T-shirts. Apparently, we didn't get the memo that it was International Gay Day at Disney World. As it turned out, there were around 77,000 openly gay people and a few hundred of us that didn't know this was happening. My wife and I decided that we would approach the day with an open mind and prove our tolerance to ourselves and to them. The end result was, I have never been exposed to such lewd speech and grotesque public displays in my entire life. We felt so sorry for the families that unknowingly brought their children there. I would have been equally appalled had heterosexuals acted that way. I don't want to even put in print the things we saw and heard.

It brought out a few points to me. First, if straight people wanted an International Straight Day at Disney World, could we pull that off? Never. Thinking back, the looks of pity on the faces of the Disney people as we purchased our tickets now speak volumes. They really would have liked to tell us what was happening in the park that day, but they were likely forbidden to do so. They wouldn't have had to say, "Stay away." They could have simply told us of the ensuing event. But someone could have been offended. Another point was the behavior these people felt justified to exhibit. All societies have standards of conduct, based on moral principles, if they are to survive. They did not exist in that park that day. But they got away with it—preferential treatment. On any other day, if you or I were to try those things, security would have ejected us from the park and rightly so.

It seems that the moral majority is no longer allowed to have freedom of opinion in most things. I'm a white, male Christian. Funny, I don't often think of myself in those terms. I think of myself as a hard-working American and as a husband and father who is proud to be a Christian. There are many who would vilify me for those things. I can't help my ethnic background, nor does it define me. I'd like people to judge me by the content of my character and not for the color of my skin.

I'm now to the point where I'm not so worried about being tolerant. While that is still important, I'd actually like to be tolerated as well! I have an opinion. On most things it's the same opinion as the majority of Americans. Opinions are actually not evil things to have. If you don't agree with me, fine. But be tolerant of me having an opinion, and I'll do the same for you. So, I'm going to have Christmas on December 25. Don't be offended. If you don't celebrate it, that's alright. I'll tolerate your holidays when you have them. I'd really like your holidays off of work, by the way. After all, non-Christians never complain on December 25 that they get to stay home from the office.

Some in this country have even complained about wearing a United States flag, shirt, or pin. They don't even want us flying the flag. We might offend someone not from this country. This is *our* country! If they don't like it, they are welcome to leave. I had the pleasure of living in South Korea for a little less than two years earlier in my life. I was not offended by their flag or their patriotism. I expected it and even encouraged it. People should support their homeland. While many have repeated the following statement in one form or another, the roots trace back to Confucius, who said: "He who takes offense when none was intended is a fool; he who takes offense when offense is intended is a bigger fool."

I couldn't agree more.

Alexander Hamilton once said, "Those who stand for nothing fall for anything." I believe that to be true. Fence sitters can easily fall the wrong direction. True commitment is more than just words. It is defined by action. Too many people don't dare voice or even form an opinion because they don't want to be labeled as intolerant by the extremist crowd. Statesman, author, and philosopher Edmund Burke's famous quote applies here as well: "All that is necessary for evil to succeed is that good men do nothing."

That is what political correctness has done for society. Common sense is all too often silenced while evil rages.

But what about being—dare I say the word—*judgmental*? That's the most effective word in the PC police's arsenal. We mustn't judge others; judging is bad. Wrong. Judging without enough information is bad, or more to the point, stupid. But judging is something we all do and must do to survive. We judge where we want to live, if our kids' friends are a good influence, and if it's safe to go to a certain place. Even some who quote the Bible don't understand Christ's meaning when he said, "Judge not that ye be not judged." I do not believe for one second that he wanted us to never form opinions and never use wise judgment. He did so many times. Yes, I know, he is the Savior and perfect, and we are not. But he also did much of what he did as an example to us. Our whole justice system is set up to judge. We simply want both sides of the story to be heard before a decision is made. That's sound advice and what I believe the Lord meant in the Bible. Making a judgment is not intolerant. If done thoughtfully, it is the right thing to do. Those who beg for tolerance need to be tolerant of those who think differently than they do. It's really just that simple.

But I'm not as discouraged as you may think. I'm just a bit frustrated, as you can probably tell. My strain of optimism stems from the fact that life is not all in the gray area. There really is right and wrong, good and evil. I'm a strong believer that in the end, right and good will prevail. My plan is to be on the prevailing team. I still think being tolerant is a good thing, but it does not mean I have to agree with everything and everyone. Another lesson learned.

Lesson 6

Tolerance does not mean we can't have an informed opinion. There are values worth defending.

So what do I do about it?

1. *Due diligence.* Despite my rant on still wanting to have my own opinions, I believe tolerance is a good thing, if applied correctly. It should make us each stop and think about the position others may have on a given issue before blindly following our own path. In business there is something called due diligence. It simply means doing your homework and examining something from all possible angles before moving forward. That's prudent advice that we can use in all aspects of life. Tolerance asks that we examine our views more closely and from multiple perspectives. Once that is done, a decision can be made and an opinion established.

2. *Walk the walk.* As annoyed as I get at people who demand tolerance, all the while showing intolerance toward others, it makes me stop and think. Am I one of those people too? I want to have my opinions, and

I try to make them informed ones. But do I really allow others that same courtesy? Can I really let someone else think entirely different from me and still treat them with respect? Each day is a test on this one. In each situation I come across, I try to take a brief pause to think and ask myself, am I respecting others for their opinions as I'd like them to do for me? An honest internal evaluation will keep things on the right track.

3. *Be willing to change.* Wait a minute. I just said that I want to have opinions and some things are worth fighting for, right? So what do I mean by "be willing to change?" First, let me be clear that I don't believe moral or spiritual convictions are negotiable. Those are always worth defending. But many things that may have been true when you first developed your opinion about them may have changed. For example, I spend most of my time in the high-tech arena. One thing I have learned is that absolute truth about a given technology changes about every six months. What might have been a right decision a year ago may have been supplanted by something better or the market may have moved in a new direction since the time my decision was made or my opinion was formed.

People should respect your opinions, but you owe it to yourself and to them to make sure you always have the most informed opinion possible.

Alright, another poem. I think I see a pattern here . . .

As a child my parents taught me
The difference between right and wrong.
Common sense once reigned supreme,
But the world has changed its song.

It started so innocent and subtle.
"Why can't we just all get along?"
So we gave a little here, then a little there,
But how did it go so wrong?

Good people were fine with tolerance,
But that was not the real end goal.
Tolerance led to open acceptance,
Then to dominance of society's soul.

Freedom of speech has often been misused
To protect positions rarely shared by you or me.

But if we voice an opposing view,
We've offended those with whom we disagree.

So the majority is labeled intolerant,
And the minority gets all the press.
The more they get, the more they want,
And we make do with less.

Common sense was not formed by man;
It comes from a much higher power.
The opposition may think they are in control,
While the rest of us just cower.

But the moral majority has not been slain,
Nor does it really sleep.
A storm is brewing on the horizon
As righteous indignation sets in deep.

For right is right and wrong is wrong,
No matter what the press may say.
And in the end when the war is won,
The right will rule the day.

7

FORGIVENESS

Pursuit 7

I wanted to be forgiven

Trust me. I've messed up enough in my life that I really need forgiveness. I suppose we all do. And I'm sure I'll be in steady need of forgiveness going forward. I'd like to think I learn from my mistakes, and I believe I have from many of them. Like the time I didn't give my wife a Mother's Day gift when she was pregnant with our first child. I mean, the baby wasn't here yet, right? She was quick to point out the life inside her, kicking and causing heartburn. I blew it and there was no way to fix that one. I've never missed a Mother's Day since.

But there are way too many things for which I am a repeat offender. The list is long and constant. I tune my kids out too easily. I have a tendency to finish people's sentences if they are slow talkers (and nearly everyone speaks slower than I do). I have less patience with my kids than I should when they don't listen the first time (or second or third). The list goes on. Oh, and I'm a recovering perfectionist. The quality of this book should prove I'm getting over that.

The point is, I'm in constant need of forgiveness. Especially from my wife, mostly for me just being me. She deserves a full-sized statue as a monument of her service to humanity for taking me in and keeping me from being too much of a menace to society. But she'd just point out that the monument was for my benefit, because she does not like attention drawn to her. I remember for her thirtieth birthday I rented a limousine and took out four of our closest friends to a high-end restaurant, all on me. There were two giant cakes at the restaurant, in the shape of a three and a zero, with black frosting roses and buzzards on them. I figured that I could poke fun at her thirtieth . . . it's not until you hit forty that it becomes personal.

The good news is she didn't mind the age jokes. It was the whole extravagance of what I had done that was at issue. Again she noted that what I had orchestrated was something *I* would like, not her. There was also the fact that I was spending that kind of money; we were saving for a down payment on our next house. In the end, I used my new Corvette as the down payment. From a guy's point of view, that was a supreme sacrifice and should forgive years' worth of sins. But it wasn't really the money with her; she just wanted me to be more responsible. She had enough kids to raise without me becoming another one. Practicality was never my strong suit. But that's her strong point. So at least I was smart enough to marry someone with skills that I lack. Did I mention I'm a repeat offender? Being impractical is definitely on the list of my offenses. The more I think about it, the more screwups I can think of. It's likely I haven't earned forgiveness in many areas just yet. The woman is a saint.

Is forgiveness a bad thing? No. But I've found that excessive focus on getting forgiveness is excessive focus on *me*. So rather than trying to get forgiveness, I've discovered that forgiving others is what I really want. That sounds so simple, right? I'm in control of myself (yeah right, see the chapter on control) so it should be easy to do. Besides, it's one of those, you know, optional virtues. Not that we all shouldn't forgive, but the timing of *when* we forgive is where the optional part comes in, or so I used to think. I'd eventually forgive everyone for everything they had ever done to me, but it would be on my terms.

Here's how this worked. When I really had been wronged, hurt, or offended, I'd go through "the process." It's a process of my own making, mind you. But I thought it was a good one. First, there'd be my shock and dismayed stage, followed by a brief period of silence. That was just to catch my breath so I could get ready for the next stage—that of righteous indignation. Then I would work my way into a nice, healthy, seething rage. Finally, after I'd told everyone I could find about how I'd been jilted, I'd grow tired of it and move on to another event. So in the end, apathy or boredom would win out more than forgiveness. Not a great system, but I thought that it worked for me.

Being a religious person, Christ's counsel about turning the other cheek seemed alright, and I thought my process kind of—sort of—met the criteria. Okay, I didn't actually analyze my plan in great detail compared to what Christ taught. He even went as far as to counsel that we should turn the other cheek a lot of times—seven times seventy to be exact. That's 490 times if you're counting. So on the 491st time, you can really go after someone, right? No such luck. The concept is actually pretty simple—forgive everyone all the time. Nice in theory, but that's not really practical, is it? I mean, what about my process? It took years to perfect and was working so well . . . or was it?

Not too long ago, there was a story in the news about a woman driving on a freeway who had a frozen turkey thrown through her windshield. She was nearly killed. After months of surgeries and agonizing pain, she had the opportunity to face her attacker, a young man. She did much more than face him; she actually pled for leniency with the judge and worked with the young man to better his life. She went far beyond forgiveness and actually changed that kid's life for the better. I think that step was missing from my original process. So why did she do it? She was completely in the right and the kid was completely in the wrong. Wouldn't she be justified in being a little resentful? The answer is no. She got it right. It became newsworthy because so few of us get it right to the level that she did.

One of the hardest things I've had to do is to truly forgive someone. That may surprise you, and I know it did me. It seems so easy to do, until you are faced with a situation where you've really been handed a raw deal. The truth is, most times we can usually find something we could have done better ourselves in a given situation. But that doesn't matter. Even if you are completely in the right with no fault of your own—like the woman with the frozen turkey—the requirement is the same. Forgive.

I finally learned why the Lord has counseled us to forgive, with no exceptions. As it turns out, I found that forgiving someone else was not such a magnanimous gesture toward the person I was forgiving; it was actually the best thing for *me*. Eighteenth century writer Samuel Johnson touches on one aspect of the reason when he stated, "A wise man will make haste to forgive, because he knows the true value of time, and will not suffer it to pass away in unnecessary pain."

There is a great deal of pain that we feel when we don't forgive. We may call it other things, such as rage, anger, or disgust, but in the final analysis, it brings us pain. My real learning experience came when I was in a situation where I was wrongly accused of something and slapped with a lawsuit. I had never felt more upset or angry in my entire life.

How could they do this? I'd done nothing wrong and I knew it! Looking back, I realize that had I communicated better with the other party, at least some of what we went through might have been diminished. In the end (which was several months later) things were resolved and we felt reasonably vindicated. Ultimately lawyers are the only ones who come out winners in any lawsuit. Your Honor, could I have another side bar, please? My brother, the lawyer, taught me that rule about lawyers always being the winners before it all started, along with another truth. That is, that no matter whether or not you win in court, it really just pushes you further down the road toward settlement. Almost always. Losers appeal and lawyers encourage it all to make more money on the billable hours. Did I mention that lawyers always win? Settlement eventually makes sense, even for winners. Otherwise the thing never ends. End side bar.

The ordeal of my lawsuit was, without a doubt, the most miserable time of my life and my family's life as well. The emotion and rage was constantly with me. It was just eating me up inside. The longer it went on, the more I realized that I was not progressing in any area of my life. I was not a better parent, husband, or business owner—nothing. In fact, I'm sure I was worse at all of them. The bitterness I felt was affecting all aspects of my existence. Even though the court case concluded, my bitterness was still there. But it had become comfortable, at least for a while. I'm sure I was as fun to be around as a network marketer who just can't wait to tell you all about their exciting "opportunity."

One day I came across a story about a man who had been wronged much worse than I. He was even imprisoned for a short time. Ultimately, he was vindicated and released. The story ends with the man on his death bed talking about how he had been wrongly accused. He never forgave the offender and lived his life in bitterness. The author of that story pointed out that the offended man's sin was worse than the original offender because he would not forgive. I realized that I would be that person if I didn't do something about it. Finally, after a few weeks of really working at it, I was able to forgive that person totally and completely. I believe he did the same with his feelings for me. What an incredible feeling to have that burden lifted from my shoulders! No more animosity, no churning and burning inside. It was all gone. Today, we are friends.

Notice that I didn't say to forgive and forget, at least not completely. I have forgotten the harsh feelings, but I remember how they ate me up inside. That has been valuable in stopping me from entering into my old process again. I've forgotten the details of the situation, but I remember what I learned from the experience and how I could have done things differently. I will never forget the event completely, and I value the experience I gained from it. Becoming a repeat offender at that level is something my family and I would not like to endure again.

The other part of not completely forgetting is that you do learn some other lessons worth remembering. If you play with a snake, for example, and it bites you, you can understand the snake and even forgive the snake. But you should still remember that it is a snake. You should be more careful the next time. Not that all people are snakes. In fact, many can and do change their ways as they grow and learn. But I'm going to be more cautious the next time dealing with that person that I've forgiven, just to avoid putting them or me in the same circumstances again. So, another lesson learned.

Lesson 7

It is much more important to forgive than to be forgiven.

So what do I do about it?

There it is, that nagging question again. Learning is one thing, but applying the lesson? That means I have to *do* things differently than I have in the past. That personal growth thing again! Well, here's what has made a difference for me.

1. *Prayer.* I know that's a religious answer, but it is what has helped me most. The key is to pray sincerely and pray about the right things. That's a little more difficult. For starters, it's not enough to pray that the Lord will help you out of the mess you find yourself in. I think we all do that to some level. But I've found when I actually prayed for the person I was having a problem with (and not just pray that they would just see things my way) it would change *me*. I would actually start to see things from their perspective. That doesn't mean I agreed with their perspective, but understanding brings peace and comfort. My prayers would also focus on my being able to forgive and not retain any bitterness. Notice that there still wasn't any praying for the problem to go away, or even for

me to get out of the situation unscathed! I've found that there are always lessons to be learned from every situation. My goal becomes to learn as much as I can, rather than just wish it all away.

2. *Focus on the long-term.* Rage and bitterness are almost always in the here and now. Even if I have truly been wronged, focusing on my long-term goals and the effect the current situation will have on those goals forces me to be more logical and rational. Often I realize that I'm blowing things out of proportion. Even if I'm not, I'm forced to look at ways to deal with the consequences of the outcome of the current event that I'm dealing with. That will help to affect the outcome in the here and now as well.

3. *Get rid of the pride.* There it is again—pride. It sure seems to rear its ugly head a lot. But the truth is, too many of us don't truly forgive someone because our pride has been hurt. Remember, we are actually the greatest beneficiary of forgiving someone else. But it must be done sincerely, honestly, and humbly. You must truly care about the other person. There is just no way to keep your pride intact if you truly forgive someone. I guess that's why it makes the headlines when someone really does it well.

To put it another way . . .

I've done so many stupid things
For which I'd like to be forgiven.
I want others to think the best of me;
Won't that make my life worth living?

Is being well thought of really so bad?
Aren't we just protecting our own reputation?
Yet being enslaved to what others may think
Is much too selfish a preoccupation.

We can't always help how others may feel,
No matter how hard we try not to offend.
But the one thing that we can be sure of,
There's something more vital on which to depend.

Rather than worrying about our own reputation
In the environment within which we live,

The one thing that should be our focus
Is that we are the ones to forgive.

There is no poison of which I'm aware
That can eat away the human soul
Like a grudge that just can't be let go,
With revenge as the ultimate goal.

To forgive at all times is the charter
With which all of mankind has been assigned.
For nothing will fill us with darkness,
Like the blackness from feeling maligned.

The forgiveness we all crave can be granted
Through the acts of our one perfect Brother.
Our task is to but live the best that we can
And to always forgive one another.

For to err is all too human,
And to forgive is quite Divine.
So if I can learn to forgive your mistakes,
Perhaps you'll do the same with mine.

8

SUCCESS

Pursuit 8

Just let me be successful!

To be honest, I've put this chapter off in my writing schedule for a while. I've always known that I really need to write it, but it's been a challenge to narrow down the topic into a logical sequence of what needs to be dealt with on this subject. The fact that I'm writing it now does not mean that I've figured all that out, as you will no doubt ascertain as you read, but it just feels like the time is right.

First, let me remind you that the premise of the book is about "things that I thought I wanted but found out in the pursuit that I really wanted something different—better, but different." When I say "I," I really mean "we" because hopefully I'm not alone in this. Hopefully, the "caught in the headlights" premise is not a surprise by now. Anyway, despite the premise, I do actually like success. My issue is more with how we define success in our lives. But before we go there, I should note that there are some folks who really don't like success. For example, socialists don't, fascists don't, and neither do communists. In short, anyone who advocates equality of outcome rather than equality of opportunity really dislikes the whole concept of success. They may claim to like success for all, but that's not success. Success involves achievement, personal responsibility, lots of hard work, and risk—all of which cause discord in an equal outcome–based society. One other group—victims (see the chapter on freedom)—fall into this category. They see the success of others, especially those who overcome great adversity to achieve it, as threatening the logic they use to justify their own situation. Since I don't consider myself in any of those groups, I'm really a success-loving kind of guy.

Not that failure doesn't have its place, mind you. I touched on this concept in the introduction, but I'll go into a little more detail here. In fact, failure is a key part of success.

None of us love failure, but it does teach us things that success doesn't. I guess that's why people like Bill Gates make me nervous. I actually like him fine; it's just that he hasn't failed enough. I don't know him personally, though he did stare at me years ago while he ate breakfast at an industry conference I was attending. It was really kind of creepy—his hair was all mashed on one side of his head from where he had slept and he just kept staring at me through the whole meal. I checked behind me and there was nothing else to look at, just me or the blank wall. Why would Bill Gates be looking at me? It must have been the wall he was interested in. Plus, that was before he had a wife to tell him that it's not polite to stare . . . but I digress.

Anyway, I have known many people who have had a great deal of success with seemingly little failure or setbacks. In every case, my humble opinion is that he or she would be a different person, a better person, if they had gone through a more, shall we say, well-rounded experience. I learned long ago that the average successful business owner has three failures before they finally hit it big. Why? Because failure teaches you things. Things about yourself and things about others around you. Success teaches things too . . . just different things. Failure teaches you what you are really made of. When the pressure is on and your world is crumbling, you begin to learn what really matters. Many things that seem to matter are now just window dressing. Family, true friends, and your relationship with God really come to the forefront. It makes you better. And hopefully, the lessons learned will temper your actions when the good times come. Learning from these experiences is critical. H. G. Wells puts it this way: "History is a race between education and catastrophe."

For most of us, we need that education to avoid future catastrophes. That's why most entrepreneurs have those three or so failures before the real success comes.

There are lessons learned from success as well. They say everyone has fifteen minutes of fame. For me it lasted for about fifteen weeks. Maybe a little less. The reason it lasted only that long is a whole different story for another book. When we launched a new product at the world's largest computer trade show, it was a hit. People waited for hours to get into the trade show booth to see what it was all about. For a brief moment, things that I said were being quoted in industry magazines and journals. I actually seemed to matter in the industry. What I found most fascinating during that time was not that I had changed but that most everyone treated me so differently. I was supposedly an up and comer in my industry and people saw me as a tool to get their own success. I had to learn a whole different set of skills for handling growth and not get pulled in too many different directions as new opportunities would arise. The challenges were very different from those brought on by failure, but still very demanding and educational.

In the introduction, I mentioned that Donald Trump was not someone who I admire. It's not that he is so successful in business that I envy him. In fact, I have more pity for him than anything else. I saw a Barbara Walters special years ago when she interviewed Mr. Trump. She talked about his lifestyle and successes, his helicopters to get around New York, and so forth. What really set me back was a comment she made almost in passing. She mentioned that his schedule was so busy that he often would not see his kids for days at a time. Think about that . . . the poster boy for success (in many people's view) had no time for his family!

The whole reason I've worked for some level of financial success was to free up more time to be with my family. If the money and power can't buy you time for what's really important, what good is it? I was certainly not surprised when Trump ended up divorced. Since that time he has gone from one trophy wife (or almost wife) to another. He may find momentary pleasure in that lifestyle, but true peace and happiness are not elements of that world. A religious leader by the name of David O. McKay once said, "No other success can compensate for failure in the home."[1]

That's a statement that I have found to be very true. The things that really matter are not financial. Success can't be measured merely by dollars and cents.

So what is a valid definition of success? What if you had Donald Trump's money but took the time to spend with family and friends; is that the ticket? Not quite. I think H. G. Wells has one of the best definitions I have found for true success: "The only true measure of success is the ratio between what we might have done and what we might have been on the one hand, and the thing we have made and the things we have made of ourselves on the other."

Success is not just parties, time off, and playing, even if it is with family. It's about potential and reaching that potential. Success involves progression—personal progression. That means a well balanced approach to life that includes family, religion, community, and work. They all matter. The catch is that when progression stops in any one area, it affects all the others.

If you avoid progression in any area, it is a step backward and not forward. We need to do the best with the hand we've been dealt. Christ teaches this principle in the parable of the talents in the New Testament. If it's been a little while since you've read it, here are the verses from Matthew 25:14–30:

> For the kingdom of heaven is as a man travelling into a far country, who called his own servants, and delivered unto them his goods.
>
> And unto one he gave five talents, to another two, and to another one; to every man according to his several ability; and straightway took his journey.
>
> Then he that had received the five talents went and traded with the same, and made them other five talents.
>
> And likewise he that had received two, he also gained other two.
>
> But he that had received one went and digged in the earth, and hid his lord's money.
>
> After a long time the lord of those servants cometh, and reckoneth with them.
>
> And so he that had received five talents came and brought other five talents, saying, Lord, thou deliveredst unto me five talents: behold, I have gained beside them five talents more.
>
> His lord said unto him, Well done, thou good and faithful servant: thou hast been faithful over a few things, I will make thee ruler over many things: enter thou into the joy of thy lord.
>
> He also that had received two talents came and said, Lord, thou deliveredst unto me two talents: behold, I have gained two other talents beside them.
>
> His lord said unto him, Well done, good and faithful servant; thou hast been faithful over a few things, I will make thee ruler over many things: enter thou into the joy of thy lord.
>
> Then he which had received the one talent came and said, Lord, I knew thee that thou art an hard man, reaping where thou hast not sown, and gathering where thou hast not strawed:
>
> And I was afraid, and went and hid thy talent in the earth: lo, there thou hast that is thine.
>
> His lord answered and said unto him, Thou wicked and slothful servant, thou knewest that I reap where I sowed not, and gather where

I have not strawed:

Thou oughtest therefore to have put my money to the exchangers, and then at my coming I should have received mine own with usury.

Take therefore the talent from him, and give it unto him which hath ten talents.

For unto every one that hath shall be given, and he shall have abundance: but from him that hath not shall be taken away even that which he hath.

And cast ye the unprofitable servant into outer darkness: there shall be weeping and gnashing of teeth.

We are all expected to do the best with the talents we've been given. There is a license plate holder that's been around for a few years that you've probably seen. It reads, "He who dies with the most toys wins."

While it is meant to be funny, there is an alarming similarity between that statement and how many people live their lives. This scripture does talk about getting an increase in our possessions, but not about getting more "toys" for ourselves. It completely misses the point of what Christ teaches. We all have different skills, resources, and abilities, and we should make the most of them. When our lives have reached an end, we will not be judged by how much we have accumulated. Rather, we will be judged by how much we did with what we were given, not just for us, but for others as well. And if you read through the chapter about serendipity again, you'll be reminded that we are each given more than we realize.

Life is not about just getting the good life and kicking back. Nor is it about being obsessed with getting more and more. It is about the legacy we leave with others. The help we provide others along their path will have much more to do with our own personal success than anything we do for ourselves.

I have a friend that I've known for many years. I'll call him Brian (mostly because that's his name). He is one of the strongest examples of success I've ever known. He is a busy man. Brian is a very gifted photographer, designer, writer, and more. He and his wife raised ten (yes, that's not a typo, I said ten) children. Years ago he and his wife made the decision to forego the lucrative career his skills would provide and help start and run a youth-oriented magazine for his religion. The pay has not been substantial and he had to take in some other jobs on the side to make ends meet. The magazine has been a huge success in terms of affecting young people for the better all over the world. Through it all, he still took time to pursue other fun activities, such as hot air ballooning (which is how I met him), that could involve his family. One day as I was visiting at his home, I noticed the huge vegetable garden in his yard. I made the comment that I couldn't believe with his schedule that it made sense for him to raise vegetables. His comment to me was that he wasn't raising vegetables, he was raising children. The garden was a way to get the kids away from friends, music, and other distractions and get some one-on-one time with one parent or the other. As they worked, they would open up and talk. "As they talk with my wife or me, it changes them. They learn from us and they know we love them. They become better people." That is true success.

Balance, perspective, service, and doing the most with what you've been given in all areas of your life is what success is all about. Success measured on those terms is harder to find but well worth the pursuit. My lesson learned was not that I didn't want success, just that my definition was all wrong in the beginning.

Lesson 8

Success is not defined by fame or fortune, but by personal progress and meeting your potential.

So what do I do about it?

1. *Set proper goals.* There is an old saying that he who fails to plan, plans to fail. There is a lot of truth in that. It is rare that someone accomplishes much without setting goals and planning ways to achieve those goals. In its more simple definition, success is often defined by the achieving of goals. I've learned that to obtain true success, I've got to start by setting proper goals. Rather than goals based on money or fame, goals should be set on developing something that will really help others. In the process, the cash and notoriety may come or may not, but they don't define me or the success I'm working to achieve.

2. *The journey is the reward.* That's actually the name of a book I read years ago about the founder of Apple, Steve Jobs. While there's a great deal about his early years that I would never want to emulate, his understanding of this principle has always stuck with me. Rather than only

focusing on a goal, it is important to take time to enjoy and appreciate the little things that happen along the way. I talk a lot about this is in the next chapter, so to avoid being redundant, I'll stop here. You can hardly wait to read the next chapter now, right? Don't answer that!

3. *Focus on the success of others.* It's very difficult to help others become successful without achieving success for yourself along the way. Of course, as I apply many of the principles in this book, the less I care about my own success, and the more success seems to follow. There's that old paradox of life, finding myself by losing myself. Success is most often had by those who help others meet their own goals.

To put it another way . . .

I know I'll never be wealthy;
I'll just never be dealt that card.
Because if I had lots of money,
I'd simply stop working so hard.

With financial concerns behind me,
I'd ensure that my life would still count.
By doing even more worthwhile things
Not tied to a dollar amount.

I'd invest a lot more time and money
Into people instead of banks.
Rather than dividends or compound interest,
My reward would be a simple "thanks."

I'd make no excuses to my children
For games missed because meetings ran late.
No matter how much my family needs my attention,
They could count on me clearing my slate.

But for most of the rich in this world,
That's not how they spend all their hours.
They're busy amassing more fortunes
To build up their ivory towers.

Many people dream of the life

That the other half all seem to live.
But happiness isn't found in more money;
It's found in the time that we give.

So, though I may never have money
Or riches for the world to admire,
I look at the lives of those with it
And see that's not what I desire.

When I get caught up in the rat race,
Where power and greed often lurk,
I remember that while on their deathbed,
No one wishes they'd spent more time at work.

Notes

1. David O. McKay, *Improvement Era* (Intellectual Reserve, Inc., 1964), 445.

9

THE BIG EVENT

Pursuit 9

If my ship would just come in

I'm a dreamer. I suppose most entrepreneurs (or entremanures) are. If you knew my mother, you'd marvel that I turned out this way. She loves her children very much, but she is very grounded. She would say she's a realist. She likes to keep her feet firmly planted on terra firma. I once asked her why she was that way, even when it came to her kids. After all, most parents would tell their kids they could do anything. She said that she was trying to protect her kids from getting their hopes built up and then getting disappointed. I can see her point of view, and I'm glad I wasn't blindly told I was the world's best at everything, only to humiliate myself in public performances where everyone could see the folly of that statement except for me. There needs to be a happy medium in there somewhere. Gratefully, my mom did encourage me in the areas where I actually showed some promise. Maybe she got it right more than I realized.

But the dreaming . . . that definitely came from my father. He's an accountant who has a true entrepreneurial spirit. I know that's an oxymoron, but it's true. The accounting side of him always kept him in a stable job throughout his life so he could provide for his family. Speaking as one of those who was provided for, I really appreciated that. On the side, however, he would dream up all sorts of businesses and give them a try. Some would work, and some . . . not so well. The ideas were always sound, but sometimes other people would let him down. He always tried to see the best in people. That can bite you at times, but I believe that a life where you trust no one and look for the worst in people is a miserable existence.

My tendency to be a dreamer was not tempered by the practicality of an accounting background. I'm the more dangerous type. Some dreamers just dream but never really commit themselves to pursuing their dream. That's fairly safe dreaming. Then there are those who get paid to dream. Many in academia often fall in this category, particularly on the college level. They don't really produce a product, and their graduate assistants do most of their work. They think, philosophize, and dream. Some of them may go too far in their dreaming, but that's another story. Anyway, as I said, I'm the more dangerous type because I act on my dreams. I tend to jump in with both feet once I've formulated a plan. If things work out—great. But if they don't, there are consequences to be dealt with. Sometimes they are financial, and at all times they are emotional. My wife is much more levelheaded but still supports most of my ventures. Did I mention that she's a saint? That or she's a glutton for punishment. I choose to believe the former.

The whole dreaming thing can be good and bad. On the plus side, without the dreamers of the world, no innovation would take place. Every large company and every great product or idea was once someone's dream. And most of the dreamers dealt with a lot of skepticism along the way. On the down side, not all dreams become a reality. In fact, most don't. That's a tough roller coaster ride of ups and downs for those that venture out in pursuit of their dreams. There is one other issue that comes up for most dreamers and even a few people who would not place themselves in that category. I call it the big event theory. Sort of like the big bang theory. Except there is no science involved.

The big event theory is fairly simple. Something really, really, really big is going to happen and life will all be better. Here are a few examples of what I mean. If your dream is music, it may be the big record contract with a major label, or being discovered by a major celebrity. *American Idol* and other talent search programs are the basic fulfillment of the big event theory for a very select few. We all love it because it feeds the dream gene in all of us. In business, it may be the VP level job or a major contract with Wal-Mart. In writing, it's to be on Oprah's book club list. The big event is what drives most of us. But for the vast majority of dreamers, it drives us . . . crazy (a very short trip for yours truly), because the big event never comes. For each *American Idol* winner, there are millions who are not so fortunate.

For me it has been even more frustrating. The big event looms ever closer. It's kind of like trying to get from the front door of my house to my mailbox by cutting the distance in half each time. I'm always making progress, but I'll never actually get there. I keep hoping that I can still get close enough to the mailbox to stretch and open the lid. Maybe I can just cheat the system a little while no one is paying attention.

The real danger in the big event theory is not just in the frustration. It's in the distraction. I can't remember how many times I've told myself things such as, "As soon as that big contract comes in, I can relax and spend more time with my family." You can plug in any big event that you would like at the beginning of that statement and any other neglected part of your life in at the conclusion. The result is the same—the big event can suck life away from you. Life that you can't get back . . . even if your ship does come in. I've even felt like I didn't deserve to enjoy other aspects of my life until the big event transpired. I've been a repeat offender on this issue, no doubt.

Finally, after anticipating big event after big event, I noticed a few things. The first was that even if the event never happened, I would still wake up the next morning and life would go on. The other thing I discovered was that life—real, meaningful, lasting life—was rarely tied to a big event at all. Okay, a few exceptions to that rule . . . marriage, the birth of a child, and the Super Bowl, but not many others. Living life is much more about the small stuff—the little events that happen day by day and hour by hour.

In fact, the things that matter most are typically the easiest to push aside in favor of that which *seems* to be really important and urgent at the moment. My kids are seemingly easy to push off when an important meeting pops up last minute. But that kid's play at school or those few moments playing ball in that backyard will have a lasting impact on that child. He will know he was a priority to you. How many of us actually treat those times with the family as though they are critical meetings that simply can't be missed? If you're like me, you get it right some of the time, and other times you just blow it. It's a constant battle.

When I finally realized that the everyday things were what mattered most, I began to change. I actually began to view those everyday events as though they were bigger events than they used to be. Those short conversations, or walks around the block with a family member, or the time spent at the dinner table with family are more important. They are no longer getting in the way of my big event; they are becoming my big events.

While life may have a few big moments that are definitely worth anticipating and planning for, you can usually count them on one hand. The little moments happen every single day (remember the whole serendipity rant a few chapters back?). So the choice is up to each of us. We can place portions of our life on hold, waiting for the few pivotal events, or we can live each day to its fullest by appreciating the small but important things that come our way. The funny thing is, if we choose the latter approach, the big events don't go away. They may even happen better than they would have otherwise, because of the way we lead our lives. Others tend to gravitate to those that enjoy living. When that occurs, good things are bound to happen. That leads to my next lesson.

Lesson 9

We should not focus on one big event to make our lives what we want them to be. The little things are what make life meaningful.

So what do I do about it?

1. *Plan but don't over plan.* I've mentioned planning quite at bit so far, but it should be mentioned that over planning is as dangerous as not planning at all. I'm still a big fan of planning; it's how we ensure we're progressing. But the funny thing is, the small events in life that really matter often come in those unplanned moments. If my schedule is too packed, I'll miss the small stuff. Meaningful existence is built on a foundation of small stuff. Not unimportant, wasteful time killers, but personal, one-on-one moments that can make a real difference.

2. *Don't define your life by one consuming event.* This is a tough one for me. If there is a large event looming, like the release of a product, a pending contract, or the like, it's very difficult to not abandon other aspects of my life because I'm stressed about the coming event. I've found over the years that there is always a coming event, so I've had to get better at fitting in the other, seemingly less urgent but very important things into my life. One dimensional living can and will cause burn out. The people that seem most satisfied with life are those that are busy in all aspects of life.

3. *Look for other events.* Another old saying is that the time to look for a new job is when you don't need one. That principle is not just for job

hunting. If I'm able to focus on the key areas of my life simultaneously, I notice that there are many events that I look forward to. When I have more than one event looming, I get less stressed about any particular event and tend to perform better in all areas. Getting too one dimensional also makes me become too desperate and anxious about the one event because I've simply put too many eggs in one basket. Diversity brings balance and level-headedness. Desperation is never a desirable trait.

To put it another way . . .

There are those that go through life
Living only for the big event.
That pivotal moment that will validate
All the time they've spent.

In that moment true joy will come,
And peace and comfort will abound.
They'll make up for opportunities lost
And feel like heaven is all around.

But waiting for the big event
Is filled with great frustration.
Too often events don't work out
No matter how grand the inspiration.

When dreams are not realized,
Anxiety is sure to set in.
There are regrets for time wasted
And for what might have been.

Big events are few and far between
If we ever really get them.
Between the stress and frustration
They'll consume you, if you let them.

For time is of such great value;
It is by far our greatest gift.
The more of it that is enjoyed,
The less we feel adrift.

We should filter our view of each day,
Using proper priorities for our screening.
Then we realize what matters most,
And life takes on greater meaning.

The kiss of a child or a talk with a friend
Seem to take on a greater role.
While the big event may still be in view,
It's no longer what makes us whole.

10

THE PERFECT BODY

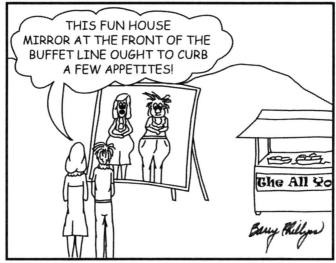

Pursuit 10

If I could just have that perfect body to make women swoon and men tremble

Stop right there. If you think I'm about to blather on about how you really don't need to get in shape, forget about it. I'd just like to bring a little sanity to the subject and help to set some reasonable expectations. In my regular life, I head up a company that provides online wellness programs for corporations, so this is a subject I actually know a little about. Not much really, but compared to my aimless ramblings in previous chapters you've already suffered through, on this—I'm an expert. So, before I get to the sanity part, let me set the stage.

In the United States and elsewhere, health care costs are skyrocketing. Health care premiums rise at 10 percent to 14 percent annually despite the fact that companies are frantically shifting costs to their employees. Managed Health Care (like HMOs) didn't even make a dent in the costs. They just didn't work. Why? Are all the doctors and hospitals just abusing patients with exorbitant fees? While the medical community is not starving, that is not the answer. The real reason for expensive health care is you and me. Managing the system doesn't work if the users of the system are out of control. And our society is out of control in many ways.

First is the fact that some people will sue at the drop of a hat. They are actually hoping for anything to go wrong so they can sue. And our legal community is constantly adding fuel to the fire. A recent national survey asked people, "What's the best way to make a lot of money?" An alarming number of people responded to sue someone. Apparently there's something wrong with actually *earning* money.

The second reason for high costs is the lifestyle that most of us lead. It's our own fault. We're just not responsible consumers. Insurance will pay our costs, so what do we care? Over half of the deaths that occur each year can be attributed to poor lifestyle choices. Tobacco, diet, inactivity, alcohol, sexual behavior . . . you know the list. According to the *Journal of Occupation and Environmental Medicine,* 50 to 70 percent of all diseases are associated with health risks that can be prevented. The single biggest culprits are physical inactivity, smoking, and obesity. We seem to live in a world that focuses on fixing us once we are broken but does almost nothing to prevent the problem in the first place. Even in my industry of wellness, which deals with prevention and healthy lifestyles, many do not want to face the real problems. We are fat and sedentary. Our ancestors would be amazed that in order to get healthy, we actually pay to go to a gym to work out. No doubt they would have gone out and worked in the yard or their community to keep active.

And then there is the food. It's one of my favorite subjects. I actually have a neighbor who really doesn't care for food. He eats because he has to in order to survive. I hate him . . . the skinny little . . . but I digress. On the other hand, there is me. I love food and I love to cook. I'm very good at both, and that's not a good combination. I constantly fight to keep the size of the food blister growing over top of my rock hard abs in check—okay, you can stop laughing. Sometimes I do better than other times. I suspect most of us are like that. If you are reading this and you're in your twenties, you may not understand. You may even think it won't happen to you. Just wait. It gets to nearly all of us as our metabolism slows down. It's just one of the many gifts of getting older. If it doesn't happen to you, then you are one of the lucky ones. But people like me will ridicule you and attempt to make you feel bad so we can feel better about our own miserable selves . . . so you'll still have to deal with it. Did I say that out loud? Anyway, we have so much unhealthy food around that is so easy to get that our challenge is much greater than at any time in history.

So what are we to do, sue McDonald's? No. Believe it or not, we have the right to choose *not* to eat that stuff. It wasn't too long ago that fast food was not so prevalent in our society. People actually cooked food in their own kitchens and stayed at home to eat. Of course, that would mean getting the family together nightly and talking about each family member's lives . . . we can't have that side affect, now can we? The truth is, if we would cook for ourselves more often—and I mean real cooking from scratch, not just throwing ready-made food into the oven or microwave, we'd eat healthier. We'd actually see the amount of butter, fat, salt, and sugar we are consuming and we'd do something about it.

There are lots of diets out there to be sure, and many of them will work if you stick to them. My personal favorite is the one where you eat five or six small meals a day, but the portions can be no bigger than your fist. I found that I kept looking for exercises to increase my fist size . . . probably not what I was really supposed to do. The truth of the matter is that if you eat healthier foods in smaller portions and combine that with some exercise, it's something you can actually live with.

So, enough on the guilt trip that you've likely heard before. While it's all true, it's still not fun to have it thrown in all of our faces. But, there is another side of this equation that also bears a little scrutiny. Have you ever seen the commercials on television for exercise equipment? You know, the ones where they have people using the machines who have absolutely perfect bodies? The men are bulging in the right places and really do have rock hard abs. The women all curve in the right places and have no body fat. You're with me, right? Let me point out a few things about those commercials that you may or may not have noticed. First, those people are all in their twenties. Second, if they really got to look that way from twenty-minute workouts three days a week, I'll eat my . . . well, they really didn't get to look that way in that amount of time. Third, for some of them, there's been more than a little enhancement from a surgeon to get a shape like that, to be sure.

Feeling a little better yet? The truth is, I'm one of those people who actually doesn't mind working out. I'm not obsessed by any means, but I kind of like it. I feel better. As a result, I usually get up very early in the morning and drag myself to the gym. I've gotten to know some of the people there, some of whom actually look like those people on the commercials. It really does take a lot of work—like a couple of hours per day. It usually takes a little surgery as well, especially for women who have had children, to maintain that shape. But there is something else I've observed. Most of these people (not all) focus a great deal of time on just themselves. They look inward rather than outward to others. Okay, they look outward at the mirrors in the gym a lot, but you know what I mean. They are obsessed with themselves. They are compulsive about what they eat, their workout time, usually their clothes, and so forth. After all, you don't put that much into it without wanting to show off the results, right? They are just too extreme. To maintain the level of expectations they have set for themselves is very self-consuming.

There is another element to consider as well. Most people who love extreme running, weights, triathlons, or whatever, pay a price. Not right away, but they do pay a price in the long run. They wear their bodies out. Many runners destroy the cartilage in a knee or ankle. Weight lifters destroy their backs or joints or even their muscle tissue. Alright, enough on the rationalization side of the argument.

As with most things in life, it is really about balance. We all need to eat healthy. But to say you will never eat chocolate again is not realistic for most of us. I mean, even if you live longer without chocolate, what would be the point? Life with no chocolate at all? Please. Ding Dongs are the nectar of life. At least I'd like them to be. Mark Twain put it this way: "Part of the secret of success in life is to eat what you like and let the food fight it out inside."

A little bit of that is not such a bad thing, I suppose. And if you say you'll never do that, it's just too depressing. We all need exercise too, just not a triathlon every other week. As we age, we should adjust our expectations. I've had to realize that I will not look like I did in my twenties. Gravity has taken its toll. But I'm not giving up either. I can still be healthy and fit; I just can't live up to the Hollywood depiction of what I should look like. The same goes for my wife. She brought five beautiful kids into the world and is still raising them. If I expect her to have the look of a supermodel, she'd have to ignore her real life for several hours a day to make that a reality. It's not going to happen and I don't even want it to happen. We all need to do the best we can and make a real effort in this category, but relax a little and don't let it dominate your life.

I know there are a few legitimate exceptions out there of people who are just really in good shape and don't have to do too much to stay that way. You've been blessed and none of this conversation really applies to you. I hate all of you . . . nothing personal. That brings me to the final lesson in this book:

Lesson 10

We should be fit and healthy, but don't go nuts over it all.

So what do I do about it?

1. *Make a real effort, but expect imperfection.* It used to be that I would start a workout program, do well for a week or two, and then slip up. Once I'd fallen off the fitness bandwagon for a day or two, or even a week, I was too depressed to go on. I see this at the gym where I work out. Every January we get the New Year's resolution crop of people wanting to get in shape. Every February, it's pretty much back to just the regulars showing up. A few people may make it into the regulars category, but most don't. So how do I hang on? Do I just have an iron will? I wish that were true, but honestly, I just lowered my expectations for myself. Not that I'm content being a slug, but I don't beat myself up if I miss a day or two—I expect that I will.

My goal at the gym is five days a week. Some weeks I make it all five days, but often I don't. Typically I get in four days. But some weeks, life gets in the way and I'm down to three. I even get down to just two days every now and again, but rarely that few because my body won't let me. Through consistency, I've discovered that my body actually *wants* the exercise. I look forward to going—especially if I've missed a day or two. So I shoot for five, I'm happy with four, not stressed over three, and my body just won't let me go below two. The point is, I'm not stressed or depressed by missing, and I look forward to going because I don't put the pressure on myself that I once did.

2. *Eat right but real.* There are those that can swear off their favorite fattening foods. I applaud them, but I'm *not* one of them. Moderation in all things is a good motto here. I try to eat what I like, but less of it. I also try not to eat in the later evening hours. That can help quite a bit. Again, I'm not perfect at this by any means, but when I follow these guidelines, I feel better, I look better, and I'm more confident.

3. *Set a target event.* Not an all consuming event (see the last chapter), but a milestone I can look forward to. When I first started working out a few years back, my motivation was to not suffer the pain and embarrassment I had felt when I went hiking with my then sixteen-year-old son, his

friends, and some of the fathers. I was amazed that I was so out of shape. I set a goal to be able to go hiking, minus that shame. Eventually we went on a vacation where hiking in a national park was on the agenda. I was thrilled that I not only kept up but felt great! I didn't obsess over the goal, but I did consistently chip away at it and have fond memories of my personal accomplishment.

To put it another way . . .

We live in a fast generation;
Fast cars, fast pace, and fast food.
With all our modern conveniences,
You'd think we'd be in a great mood.

But life has become more stressful,
While our physical activity is on the decline.
We tend to eat lots of fries and a burger
As we rush to make an appointment on time.

And then there are all those desserts
Just waiting around every turn.
Even if you swear, "No more donuts!"
Your boss hands you one out of concern.

Eventually you go buy a gym pass
To stop the mudslide that is your physique.
As you look at the hard bodies around you,
You know your chance for success is quite bleak.

You lack sufficient time and motivation
To achieve that body by riding a bike.
And even if you put all that time in,
It's the looming diet you really dislike.

Yet, if you think of all those people
In your life that you really admire.
It's not likely because they look good
There's more that causes them to inspire.

While your character is most important,
Being healthy is important too.
There is more to life than physical appearance,
But without health there's not much you can do.

So taking care of yourself is essential;
Exercise and diet must be in control.
But realistic expectations are also required
Or you'll go nuts while meeting your goal!

BRINGING IT HOME

By now you've no doubt noticed a pattern in the ten things that we pursue and then find out that they're really not what we're after. In the end, the most compelling thing that we really want is not happiness or success or any of the other things we've discussed. At least not by the standard definitions most people go by. What we really want is peace. That feeling that we are on the right path, doing the right things, and our relationships are all intact. It sounds so simple but takes a lifetime to achieve. All the other things talked about in this book directly or indirectly affect our ability to obtain it.

In our society there are so many pressures, opportunities, and choices placed before us, it seems overwhelming at times. We live at a faster pace with more demands on our time than ever before. Each generation faces its own epic struggle. Our generation may face the greatest challenge of all—to balance our time and sift through all of those things that are enticing but not important to finding peace in our lives.

There is a common thread or litmus test that we can use as a guide to finding peace. It is that selfishness that is the anti-peace. There are many things that sound attractive that cause us to focus on ourselves. The more we do those things, the more we come up feeling empty—wanting. On the other hand, if what we are pursuing is selfless and for the betterment of others, we're on the right path. Why does it work this way? My personal belief is that we all have what I call a spiritual DNA. The spiritual gene pool we draw from comes from our Creator. As his children, we are a lot like him, or a least we have the potential to be more like him. The only way we can really get the peace we seek is to follow his example. There are no shortcuts, no "get peace quick" schemes.

Life is full of paradoxes. The greatest one is that we must lose our lives to find our lives. But losing our lives is not of much value, unless the "losing" is done the right way. We must lose our lives in being in the service of others and in God's service as well. I've come to believe they are one and the same.

There are many pursuits we each have in life. These chapters contain only ten of the ones that most of us think will bring happiness, but they really do not. As we pursue them, we find out that there is something different and better we should have been after in the first place. There are many more that fall in the same category which are far too common, and we each have our own customized list as well. Life's road is difficult enough without constantly taking wrong turns along the way. As we really understand what our long term objectives are, we tend to pursue the right things in the first place.

I hope you have taken away something from these pages that has made you think and even laugh once in a while. And if by chance you avoid getting caught going after the wrongs in your life, so much the better. But that's probably too much to ask for. After all, if I figured this stuff out, you probably knew it all years ago.

About the Author

Barry K. Phillips is the proud father of five children and the husband to one patient, long-suffering, patient, understanding, patient wife. He is the cofounder and president of PrimeWellness, Inc., a technology company that creates online health and wellness centers. Barry has consulted and trained extensively with *Fortune 500* companies in the areas of leadership, mentoring, problem solving, decision making, public speaking, and more. He has authored or coauthored several training courses in those same areas that are still used in corporate America today. Formerly, Barry was editor-in-chief for an international computer magazine. He has also written for Glenn Beck's *Fusion* magazine and contributes regularly to politicalderby.com.

Barry enjoys writing, cooking, hot-air ballooning (contrary to popular belief, he does require a burner to create the hot air), woodworking, sports, and spending time with his family—apparently, they're tired of changing the locks.